DAVID LOW

Colin Seymour-Ure and Jim Schoff

SECKER & WARBURG
LONDON

First published in England 1985 by
Martin Secker & Warburg Limited
54 Poland Street, London W1V 3DF

British Library Cataloguing in Publication Data

Seymour-Ure, Colin
   David Low.
   1. Low, David, *1891-1963*   2. Cartoonists –
   New Zealand – Biography
   I. Title   II. Schoff, Jim
   741′.092′4   NC1761.L6

ISBN 0-436-44755-X

Filmset in Monotype 12pt Bembo
and printed in Great Britain by
BAS Printers Limited, Over Wallop, Hampshire

Contents

To the family and friends of David Low

Preface

This is the first full-length book produced in the Centre for the Study of Cartoons and Caricature at the University of Kent. Its preparation would have been impossible without the cooperation of the Low family. Low left a large collection of papers: drawings, sketchbooks, notebooks, letters, photographs, press cuttings. (Not only did he keep the cuttings – he stuck them methodically into scrapbooks, seventeen in all.) The authors' first debt is to Low's daughters, Mrs Prue Rowe-Evans and Dr Rachael Whear, for their generosity in letting us work through this material. They provided help in many ways ranging from cups of tea to reminiscence, and they both read the manuscript in draft and saved us from errors. We are most grateful to them and their families for their kindness and encouragement.

The book was made possible equally by the generosity of the trustees of the Leverhulme Trust. The Cartoon Centre depends almost wholly upon funds from Foundations and the income earned by research fees and touring exhibitions. In 1973 the Nuffield Foundation made a grant to Dr G. M. Thomas, founder of the Centre, which enabled a start to be made on the work of conserving, cataloguing and indexing the cartoon originals held there. The number of these soon increased to more than 70,000 and a grant from the Leverhulme Trust in 1979 enabled the work to continue under Jim Schoff and Ms Deborah Derrick. Among the cartoons are more than 3,500 Low originals dating from his most celebrated period, the years between 1927 and 1949 when he worked on the *Evening Standard* for – one might rather say 'with', since he used his employer so often as a foil – Lord Beaverbrook. This collection was transferred to the Centre by Mr A. J. P. Taylor when the Beaverbrook Library in Fleet Street of which he was Honorary Director was dispersed. In 1982 the Trust made a further grant for research on the Low material under the direction of Professor Colin Seymour-Ure. The bulk of the grant went to continue the post of Research Fellow/Administrator held by Mr Schoff and to employ Ms Liz Ottaway as Research Associate. Professor Seymour-Ure, further, was enabled to take a term's leave of absence to work on the project full-time. This book and an exhibition of Low's work at the National Portrait Gallery (most of the exhibits of which are reproduced here) are among the first products of the research. The Centre's debt to the Leverhulme Trust is considerable; and the authors have appreciated the personal interest taken by the former Director, Dr Ronald Tress.

Colin Seymour-Ure is grateful, too, to the Warden and Fellows of Nuffield College, Oxford, especially David Butler and Jim Sharpe, for enabling him to spend the Michaelmas Term of 1984 there while writing the first draft of the manuscript; and to Ted and Julia Whybrew for their hospitality at Rousham. A wide range of people – visitors to the Cartoon Centre, our families, correspondents who replied to requests for information – have helped us along the way. Among librarians and archivists we are particularly grateful to Jim Andrighetti at the State Library of New South Wales, Anne Gray at the Australian War Memorial, Barbara Perry of the Australian National Library, Dr Angela Raspin of the London School of Economics, and Jill Tasker of the Library at New Zealand House. Professor Peter Mellini and Dr Adrian Smith have taken a particular interest while carrying on research of their own about Low. John Jensen kindly read the manuscript with a professional eye and forestalled some non-professional absurdities. At every stage we have benefited from the wisdom of Graham Thomas and the efficiency of Liz Ottaway. The quality of the reproductions in this book owes much to the meticulous skill of the University of Kent's photographer Jim Styles, who always produced the best available image from a daunting range of cartoons. Thanks go, too, to Mark Bryant, our editor at Secker and Warburg and Sue Hadden, the designer, for the care with which they saw the manuscript through to publication.

In the preparation of the book Jim Schoff has been responsible for tracing material, making an initial selection of drawings and a first draft of many of the captions; while Colin Seymour-Ure wrote the text and bears responsibility for the contents of the anthology as a whole and for errors and inadequacies. We hope the result is a volume of which Low would have approved, or which he would have felt, at the very least, in a nice paradox, is not a caricature – either of himself or his work.

Canterbury, 1985

C.K.S-U.
J.S.

Introduction

Sir David Low – he accepted a knighthood in 1962 – was the most celebrated cartoonist of his age. He was born in New Zealand on 7 April 1891 and died in London on 19 September 1963. He was an established success on the *Bulletin* in Australia by his mid-twenties and on the London evening *Star* before he was thirty. Lord Beaverbrook coaxed him to the *Evening Standard* in 1927, and there he displayed a mastery of his art for more than twenty years. From 1950 to 1953 he worked on the *Daily Herald* and then for ten years, before his death, the *Manchester Guardian*. On the great international issue of the 1930s – the rise of European Fascism – he was triumphantly and tragically correct. More generally, he observed events from a left-of-centre vantage point; but he was never extreme enough, in opinion or style, to lose touch with his large (mainly middle-class) audience or to seem strident and predictable. On the contrary, he expressed with great skill the conventional wisdom of the day – for purposes, more often than not, of challenging it. Whatever the issue, domestic or foreign, Low's mockery helped his contemporaries, and can help us still, to understand the attitudes he criticised as well as those he shared. Later generations are bound to lose many of the nuances and associations of his cartoons. None the less he has surely fixed, more than anyone else, the lasting image of Hitler and Mussolini. In Colonel Blimp, too, he created an image of reactionary stupidity which has taken on a life of its own. ('Gad, Sir! Baldwin may have no brains, but he's a true Englishman.') People who look blank at the name Low will smile in recognition at the name Blimp.

But Low was more than a cartoonist. His portrait caricatures have become collectors' items, more famous than any (bar Max Beerbohm's) since the heyday of *Vanity Fair*. As an illustrator he was adept at straddling the boundaries of reality and fantasy in his depiction of real people and 'types' for topical satires by H. G. Wells and Peter Fleming. His *The Modern Rake's Progress*, originally planned as a gentle satire on the Prince of Wales' circle and with a text by Rebecca West, is crammed with recognisable figures from London life in the 1930s. He experimented with cinema animation. He wrote incisively on his art. He became an experienced broadcaster and essayist.

This book presents work, some of it previously unpublished, from across the full range of Low's career. It provides a commentary on his life and times, his art, his attitudes and his impact. Some cartoonists can draw, some can capture a likeness, some have a sharp political nose and are vindicated by events. As the following pages seek to show, few have been so successful in every one of these ways as David Low.

I Low's Life and Times

Low was born in New Zealand in a predominantly Scottish settlement, Dunedin, to which his grandfather had emigrated in the 1860s. One of the first signs of his aptitude for drawing, according to his mother, was a picture of a Scotsman in full dress which he drew on his nursery wall. When he was six or seven he used to paint scenery for playlets. He made his parents pay 'admission' and he used the proceeds, like the rest of his pocket money, to buy comics. *Chips*, *Comic Cuts*, *Big Budget*; these and others, shipped out from England and America, were the popular sellers of the time.

None of this sounds especially precocious. More impressive as a sign of things to come was the prolonged scrutiny which the comics received. Low did not just look at them: he carefully copied them, over and over again. He up-ended an old piano case and turned it into a 'studio'. Here, in privacy, he grappled with the problems of composition. Drawing from the stock of joke ideas which, as he saw, cropped up again and again, he started sending his own efforts to editors in London, He kept at it, and

I Self-portrait, unpublished, *c.* 1905

Obviously the result of long, hard study in the mirror, this early sketch shows a young and contemplative Low. Low, a right-hander, has not reversed the mirror's image, though the pen in his drawing hand is only suggested.

I

one day, 'I opened my *Big Budget* to find one of my own three-picture strips printed – printed in microscopic size, but printed. Victory! I leaped in the air.'[1] He was eleven years old.

From then on, to borrow the labels off two of his later cartoon characters, it was Onanonanon and Upanupanup. Today, *Big Budget*: tomorrow the world – hundreds of papers, at any rate, in tens of countries. Low's autobiography does not, of course, suggest his success was inevitable. He gives credit to chance, especially the luck of being in various right places at right times. But he credits sheer hard work as much. The picture emerges of an artist not so much struggling, in the years before he came to London, as simply working hard.

After the *Big Budget* came, at much the same time, success with a topical cartoon in a light Christchurch weekly, the *Spectator*. Then an Australian women's magazine, the *New Idea*, published his entry in a readers' competition and gave him an honourable mention. The competition ran monthly. Soon, back came the first prize. He won it half a dozen times, almost coming to rely on the five shillings prize money. Low then started doing police-court drawings for *New Zealand Truth*, a sensational weekly paper. He picked up a variety of commercial work, and the *Spectator* retained him to illustrate two jokes a week. He graduated from his piano case to a converted chicken house. He was still barely in his teens.

The next significant advance came in 1907 when Low, now sixteen, was hired at £2 a week to help illustrate the *Sketcher*, a magazine started by a local caricaturist, Fred Rayner, to mark the holding of an international exhibition in Christchurch where the Low family now lived. Next year the *Spectator* took him on full-time to draw two full-page political cartoons and four or five small ones weekly. This was a proper job. It still left time to contribute two half-page cartoons each week to a new Labour paper, the *Weekly Herald*. But this extra liaison, and his own increasingly obvious Labour sympathies, led to a row, and in 1910 Low and the Liberal-inclined *Spectator* parted company. With characteristic resource, Low promptly persuaded another Liberal weekly, the *Canterbury Times*, that his cartoons could help win a circulation war. Possibly even to his own surprise, he found himself with twice the salary, more space and better quality printing.

He was not long on the *Canterbury Times* before a cable came from the Sydney *Bulletin*: 'Can you take position as our Melbourne cartoonist for six months.' Here was real success. The *Bulletin* was nationalistic, irreverent; known throughout Australia

as 'the bushman's Bible'. A famous cartoon marking Queen Victoria's funeral conveys something of its flavour: a drunk waits glumly outside a pub, closed for the day – the caption is 'The Nation Mourns'. Above all, led by the American Livingston Hopkins ('Hop') and the Englishman Phil May (a model Low had seized on in his copying phase), the magazine had become a stimulus and nursery for artistic talent. It was the dearest wish of all black-and-white artists to get into the *Bulletin*, Low wrote. 'And into it I went for a six months' engagement. What luck!'[2]

Luck indeed: the opening arose only because a regular contributor fell ill. But Low had been preparing the ground. Each week he sent twenty copies of the *Spectator* to Australian editors. He went on holiday to Sydney before starting at the *Canterbury Times*, 'to see what kind of people ran the *Bulletin*'. 'They had been accepting a lot of my work latterly,' he wrote in his *Autobiography*, 'and one never knew where that might lead.'[3]

2 *Spectator*, Christchurch, New Zealand, *c.* 1908

A political Labour League was formed in New Zealand after the 1904 Conference of Trades and Labour Councils. This threatened the premiership of Sir Joseph Ward, leader of the Liberals who had previously represented both Liberal and Labour interests. The first Labour member was elected in the 1908 general election. To Low, Ward's 'Liberal' umbrella will afford more protection than the puny 'conservatism' of the leader of the Opposition, W. F. Massey.

Describing his start with the *Spectator*, Low later called such cartoons the work of an 'obedient hireling'.

3

3 (opposite) *Spectator*, Christchurch, New Zealand, 31 December 1909

An early example of a full-page gag. Did readers really need the numbers to help them? The influence of children's papers such as *Comic Cuts* is plain.

4 *Spectator*, Christchurch, New Zealand, *c*. February 1910

Kitchener visited New Zealand in February 1910. Premier Joe Ward figures as a medal added to his other conquests.

It is tempting to view Low's work in Australia between 1911 and his departure for England in 1919 as simply the rehearsal for the big show; all the more so since his progress had few setbacks. Only after the Second World War, arguably, did he even begin to falter, and by then he had topped the highest peaks and was in his mid-fifties. It had been Upanupanup all the way, not simply Onanonanon. In one sense undeniably it was a rehearsal. In those days Australia could not be a world stage. Still less could New Zealand: *MADE GOOD* was the unembarrassed headline of *New Zealand Truth* when its celebrated former contributor arrived in England. But the Australian years were certainly not a rehearsal

5

5 'Preparing for the fray',
Canterbury Times, Christchurch,
New Zealand, 13 September 1911

W. F. Massey, leader of the
opposition Reform Party, was a
favourite of the Conservative press.
But in the Liberal *Canterbury Times*
he is made into a woebegone Don
Quixote by Low during the election
campaign of 1911.

The *Canterbury Times* gave Low
more space, with excellent
reproduction and printing facilities.
These are the cartoons he chose to
send to Australian editors.

PREPARING FOR THE FRAY

6 (opposite) 'Some writers and
artists', *Caricatures*, Sydney, Tyrrell,
1915

'When after my travels I looked at
my four hundred portrait caricatures
collected in a book – my first real
book – I saw that, although I had
succeeded in avoiding flashy
"lightning-sketch" rubbish, my aim
at the psychological essence had
achieved, except in a very few cases,
only wooden superficiality. The
reason was clear. A good piece of
caricature represents not only what
the artist sees but what he *knows*
about what he draws. The nature of
the job had not allowed me sufficient
time to get to know enough of the
people who lived within these visible
shells.' (*Autobiography*, p. 54)

in the different sense of showing promise that was undeveloped.
Low did not learn his lines there to pipe them to England. He
piped them in Australia. In fact he delivered them full blast. When
Low left the *Bulletin*, it was news.

The six-month contract in Melbourne required Low to make
twelve topical drawings on a weekly page. Many of them illustrated ideas sent in by readers in return for payment. Low worked
hard and led a flourishing, mildly bohemian social life. At the
end of the contract he took two months off and went to Sydney.
By a decision utterly in character, he walked there – 600 miles
(though he accepted lifts for 150 of them). The Sydney Office
could not offer him a regular job but retained him 'to range the
length and breadth of Australia, transport charges but not living
expenses paid, making caricature portraits of local notables'.[4] This
suited Low splendidly and enabled him both to get to know the
country and to meet 'practically everyone of importance'. It also

6

SOME WRITERS AND ARTISTS

7 Henry Lawson, *c.* 1918

Low drew twenty-five portraits, like this one of the poet Henry Lawson, for a book of anonymous verses about well-known Australian figures in the arts (provisionally entitled *Apollo in George Street*). The publishers, Angus and Robertson, judged the verses too unfriendly to risk publication. Low's drawings, whose style clearly anticipates his caricatures of the 1920s and 1930s, remain unpublished too.

Lawson (1867–1922) was a *Bulletin* contributor famous for such classic ballads as 'The Drover's Sweetheart' and 'The Sliprails and the Spur'. Low pictures him with his notorious greeting, which signals that he needs 'threepence for a beer'.

provided the material for a book of 400 caricatures, published with great success in 1915. Sadly his best Australian caricatures (in his own estimation) were never published. These were to illustrate a book of anonymous verses about artists and writers of the

Another in the 'Lawson' series. Famous at this time for 'The Sentimental Bloke' and other ballads, Dennis was an old friend of Low's and had shared digs with him in Melbourne. Perhaps this drawing relates back to those days, when, Low wrote, '. . . Den filled in as a civil servant complete with two-inch starched collar and vest slip, an effect quite unsuited to his bony-nosed Roman face' (*Autobiography*, p. 79).

day, to be called *Apollo in George Street*. The publishers, Angus and Robertson, cancelled the book in 1919 for fear of libel.[5]

Back in Sydney in 1913, the *Bulletin* let him move in as a general cartoonist, trying his hand at everything including sport. Then

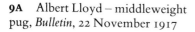

9A Albert Lloyd – middleweight pug, *Bulletin*, 22 November 1917

Low dramatises the natural power of the boxer by forcing the angle made by chest and arm hard against a solid black background, instead of using cross-hatching or shading.

9B McLaren – captain of the Queensland cricket team, *Bulletin*, n.d.

Low remarked that 'true character is not displayed in a man's physical shell but in his individual *use* of it'. Spy's static *Vanity Fair* style of depicting sportsmen has been here overtaken by a modern eye and consciousness. Low was adept at the depiction of movement. He liked to capture 'life on the wing', and he was fascinated by the potential of cinema. Note Low's characteristic instruction to the blockmaker about the position of the figure on the page.

in 1914 he was appointed resident political cartoonist in Melbourne. War had broken out. Norman Lindsay, long established in Sydney, was to do 'dramatic and allegorical war cartoons', while Low looked after 'the personalities and minutiae of politics' in Melbourne, where the Commonwealth Government was still seated during the construction of Canberra.

Low's success in the war years is epitomised in his relationship with Billy Hughes, the volatile, dominating Prime Minister of the Labour Government and its coalition successor. Hughes,

10

THE SHADOWS DEEPEN

ONE OF THEM: 'Say, for goodness sake hurry up and finish this game. There's a storm coming.'

10 'The shadows deepen', *Bulletin*, 6 August 1914

A. J. Cook (Liberal/Conservative leader) and Andrew Fisher (Labour leader) vie for prime-ministerial office while the need for strong leadership grows. Low was one of the first cartoonists to realise that the new war would drag Australia out of its bushland 'dream-time' into a wider, darkening world.

whose extravagance was accentuated by his small physique, was a natural subject for caricature. The *Bulletin* disliked his personality more than his policies, and Hughes responded with hostility. But hostility towards its cartoonists was of course grist to the *Bulletin*'s mill. When Hughes pressed for the exclusion of a Low cartoon, even though the wartime censor had passed it, the editor threatened not to bring the paper out at all, and Hughes had to back down. After that he toughened the censorship rules.[6]

11 'Coming together', *Bulletin*, 8 February 1917

Expelled from the Labour Party on the issue of conscription, Prime Minister Hughes made an alliance with his old adversary A. J. Cook and formed a Coalition Government on 17 February 1917. Low pictures the preliminary bargaining.

COMING TOGETHER

When the *Bulletin* editor, S. H. Prior, felt that the Prime Minister's office was pushing him too hard to suppress a Low cartoon, even though it had satisfied the wartime censor, he exploded. 'Then *The Bulletin* won't come out next week at all.' The threat worked: the paper duly appeared, with Low's cartoon in place.

Censor.

" The 'Bulletin's ——!! —— ? —— ! * * —— (he cut this out) —— censor in the act of putting a few finishing touches on the artists front page cartoon .

13 'Give us a spell, boys', previously unpublished, 2 July 1917

Partly as a result of brushes with the *Bulletin*, the Government tightened the censorship. Low borrows from a well-known recruiting poster to make his criticism. The hard-pressed Australian soldier is based on 'The Little Boy at Manly', invented by the cartoonist Livingston Hopkins to personify Australia as a young force in the world. The censor's verdict can just be seen near Low's signature: 'Permission to publish refused'.

Hughes' reputation provided the subject of Low's Australian *tour de force* – a drawing of Hughes fulminating in Downing Street during the Imperial Conference of 1916. This attracted the conventional marks of cartooning success. Low was showered with letters, Hughes signed copies for the British Cabinet, and the

14

the Firebrand and the Fossils

Asquith : "David, talk to him in Welsh and pacify him!"

THE FIREBRAND AND THE FOSSILS

Governor-General asked for the original, which was hung for a time in the Canberra Parliament.

Such episodes made Low news. A fellow cartoonist even drew a cartoon of Hughes with Low included in it. The publication of Low's *The Billy Book* (1918) took celebrity one stage further. This was a slim, paper-covered anthology – 'a fantastic account in caricature of Hughes' adventures during his travels to and in Britain'.[7] It was intended to be light rather than malicious. But it was seized on by the Prime Minister's friends and enemies alike and quickly sold 60,000 copies. Hughes' friends saw it as new evidence of Low's personal hostility and attacked Low in the pro-Government press. Not for the last time, Low protested that political opposition need not mean personal malice.

Two other episodes showed Low's capacity to find himself in the news. One was the production by a Sydney businessman of 'Billiwog' glove puppets, based on a cartoon in *The Billy Book*.

14 'The Firebrand and the Fossils' ('The Imperial Conference'), *Bulletin*, 16 March 1916

Hughes fulminates in the Cabinet room at Downing Street during the Imperial Conference of 1916. Asquith appeals to Lloyd George (a Welsh speaker) to pacify him. Balfour and Grey cringe. The cartoon was a sensational success which took Low by surprise.

'I spent three days on this drawing and when I had finished, it looked to me overdrawn. Too full of lines . . . A slight quip should not be represented in laborious technique but with economy of line . . . I contemplated tearing it up and starting again, but there was no time, so off it went.' (*Autobiography*, p. 66)

A VISIT TO THE FRONT.

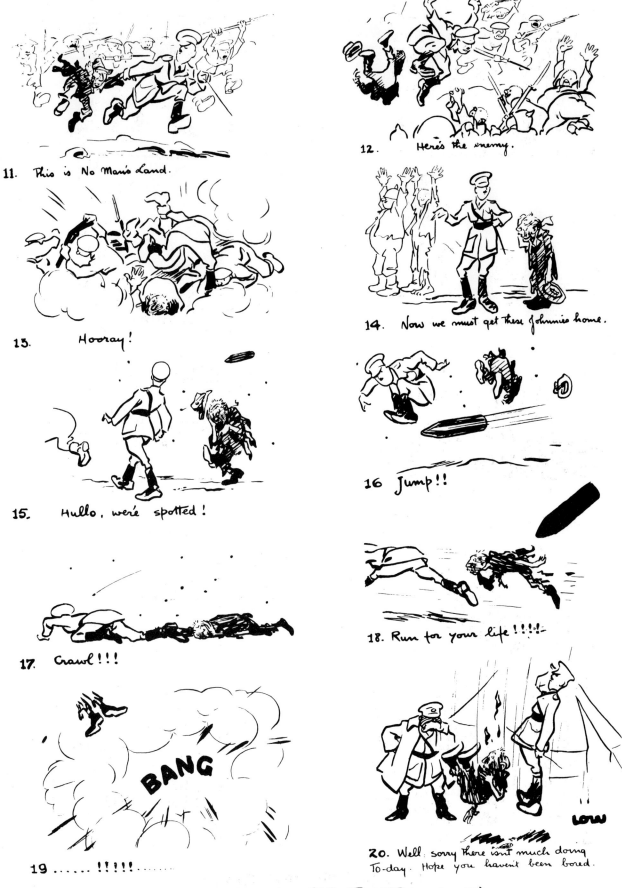

A VISIT TO THE FRONT. (CONTINUED)

15 (previous pages) *The Billy Book*, Sydney, Bookstall, 1918

This running story was more typical of the spirit of The *Billy Book* than of its format. Most of the cartoons were single-frame.

BILLIWOG

LONDON'S LATEST CRAZE

ALMOST HUMAN

BABIES CRY FOR IT

DIRECTIONS FOR USE

Blow up with wind until head expands, then release hole in face, whereupon Billy will emit loud noises until he goes flat.............

16 'Billiwog' [sic], *The Billy Book*, Sydney, Bookstall, 1918

'A Sydney trader was fired with the idea of manufacturing "Billywog", so I reduced the idea to tangible form on glove-puppet lines, modelled a head of Hughes in plasticine and sold him the puppet rights outright. In due course puppets of "Billywog" appeared around and about at Billy's comings and goings, wagging, gesticulating and mocking the indignant original according to the mood of the wearer.' (*Autobiography*, p. 77)

NO WAR IS COMPLETE WITHOUT ONE

These provoked comment in the press when flourished on public occasions – and also because they were manufactured in Japan. The other, more serious, episode was an attempt to conscript Low. Conscription had been defeated in a referendum, but after a general election Hughes tried again. He put the call-up into immediate effect, anticipating (incorrectly) a 'yes' vote in a second referendum. Some papers suggested that Low, who had not in fact opposed the conscription policy, was being called up to prevent him from cartooning. The *Bulletin* appealed for his

18

NO ESCAPING HIM

The *Sydney Bulletin* illustrates Mr Hughes welcoming the
Australian press delegates to this country

exemption on grounds of his 'national importance', and succeeded. The decision was naturally controversial.

Low launched examples of his work abroad from Australia,
just as he had from New Zealand. He sent about fifty copies of
The Billy Book to 'writers, publicists and editors' in Britain. The
Manchester Guardian, which could not afford its own cartoonist,
had been reprinting his work occasionally in a weekly feature of
cartoons from overseas. (The first was published on 4 January
1915.) As before, therefore, Low was not completely surprised
when the call to London came. The agent was Henry Stead, son
of the crusading Victorian journalist, W. T. Stead. Henry
managed *Stead's Review*, the Australian branch of the family
enterprise. Following the publication of a paragraph by the writer
Arnold Bennett in the *New Statesman* (1 February 1919), he was
contacted by the Cadbury Press, which owned the *Daily News*
and the London evening *Star*. 'If the Press-lords of this country
had any genuine imagination,' Bennett had written, commenting
on a Low cartoon in the *Manchester Guardian* of 25 January, 'they
would immediately begin to compete for the services of that cartoonist and get him to London on the next steamer.' Just how

17 'No escaping him', *Manchester
Guardian*, 25 January 1919

This is the *Bulletin* cartoon
reproduced in the *Manchester
Guardian* and spotted by Arnold
Bennett who commended it in his
New Statesman column (1 February
1919): '. . . When one thinks of the
melancholy and ridiculous efforts of
Punch in the domain of political
caricature, and of the tenth-rate
drawings in the popular dailies, one
perceives that life in Sydney must
have appreciable compensations.'
Before long Lloyd George would
similarly bring out the best in Low.

far this suggestion was cause or simply occasion is unclear. Low, by his own account, had marked out the *Daily News* as a sympathetic and likely paper and had been sending copies of the *Bulletin* regularly to the editor, A. G. Gardiner, and to Henry Cadbury. Bennett, however, would have preferred Low to join Beaverbrook's *Daily Express*. Whatever the cause, Stead negotiated terms. His enemies in the press, including the *Bulletin*'s rival, *Smith's Weekly*, wished good riddance. He bade goodbye to his busy circle of friends – artists, writers, politicians – and with his sister, who had joined him in Melbourne with his mother and younger brother, he sailed off to California and thence to England.

MADE GOOD. There he went; the beneficiary in part of good fortune but undoubtedly also of the intelligent, calculated exploitation of a natural gift. 'What does he want?' muttered J. F. Archibald, former editor of the *Bulletin*, when Low turned up one day at Norman Lindsay's house. 'Mark my words, he's after something.' 'He was ruthlessly determined to get on,' Lindsay reflected in 1950, 'and submerged all other interests to that objective.'[8] The ruthlessness – or singlemindedness, as friends might have chosen to call it – was not directed against others: Low did not try to displace his colleagues. Nevertheless, he seemed rather obviously on the make.

His drive must have rested largely on enormous self-confidence. To judge from the autobiography, it was in this more than his drawings that he was precocious. With self-confidence too came resourcefulness, individuality and practical curiosity. His home life fostered them all. His mother's chief anxiety was that her children should not grow up 'stereotyped'. Herself the object of strict parental discipline, she determined not to commit the same mistake. When her eldest son died from peritonitis, she and her husband were ready to believe he had been weakened by 'overstudy', and they removed the other children from school. Low was eleven. He thus went into adolescence without the advantages and disadvantages of a peer group. His discipline was self-discipline. As he taught himself to draw, squeezed in his piano case, or thought things through in his 'thinking ditch', he was his own critic. He learnt to argue with himself – a practice reflected in his cheerful but combative prose style and, more importantly, carried through to his cartoons, many of which contain internal dialogue. The habit of detachment, from political orthodoxies as from the crowd at a boxing ring or a political meet-

20

AT SUNNYSIDE

18 'At Sunnyside', *Spectator*, Christchurch, New Zealand, 1902

In a spoof 'auto–obituary' published forty years later, Low wrote: '. . . in 1902 [Low] published his first political cartoon, which was applauded as displaying much statesmanship. He was then aged eleven, which is about the right age for a political critic. The first cartoon, which represented the local authorities as lunatics because of their reluctance to remove certain trees which obstructed traffic and their eagerness to remove others which did not, epitomises Low's life work, for he may be said to have lived on the same idea throughout his long career, varying and adjusting it to situations as they arose.' (*Strand Magazine*, August 1942)

THE LUNATIC: 'I suppose you haven't got a tree about you I can chop
   down?'
THE VISITOR: 'No, I haven't. But why?'
THE LUNATIC: 'O, I'm the Domain Board!'

ing, must have come easily. 'Success' was to be measured, equally, by personal satisfaction not by worldly plaudits.

Fortunately young Low had a powerful curiosity, or his individualism might have been a path to self-destruction. He was an avid reader, much encouraged by his father, and became a lifelong self-educator. As a boy he plunged into the classics of history and English literature just as, in the 1930s, he boned up on Communism, Fascism and Nazism, dividing his study wall into compartments within which he pinned 'the philosophical fundamentals and working principles of each system'.[9]

The curiosity had a strong practical streak. This too was acquired from his father, who was forever trying new ideas and seeking to turn them to commercial advantage. The Lows had the latest photographic equipment, the first phonograph in Christchurch and a financial stake in the first bioscope. Low senior took young David to the race course to show him how to bet, and made him light up a pipe on his sixteenth birthday to test

21

19 USA cartoon-drawing lessons, *c.* 1900–05

'I answered an American advertisement and for some time sent a dollar a month to a correspondence school of Caricature in New York. They made it easy – too, too easy. The conventions again, the stale old dodges for evading real drawing. How to become a complete hack.' (*Autobiography*, p. 28)

As the teacher's scribbled comment shows, the school was impressed: 'Excellent. No beginner has done better.'

Lesson II

Paper

Excellent. No beginner has done better

the pros and cons of smoking. Low's walk to Sydney was in the same spirit. So too were his experiments in starving (his landlady found him lightheaded after eight days, and put a stop to it), and his test, with a friend, of the consequences of drinking a bottle of whisky straight off.

In a different way, Low found that formal instruction in draw-

22

DAVID A C LOW.
1906

20 Unfinished cartoon drawing, 1906

How many cars were on the roads of Christchurch at this time? Low may have been short of models, yet he deftly captures the leaping inevitability of the new-fangled automobile. The movement lines of the composition are clumsy and the differences of scale are too great, but the drawing shows the fifteen-year-old Low's ability to extract drama from commonplace situations.

ing did not satisfy his curiosity. At the age of thirteen he tried an American correspondence course. Then he enrolled in the Canterbury School of Art. But he found the instruction static and deadening: he wanted to draw from *life*, in the broadest and most literal senses. So he went his own way, meeting technical challenges – how to do the stereoscopic drawings for a coin-in-the-slot machine, for instance – as they presented themselves. To please his parents, who rather hoped he might follow a profession (a clergyman, his mother fancied), he went for two years to a local business college. Obviously he was intelligent; but individualism, preoccupation with drawing and lack of motivation made him fail.

21 'Off to London', *Bulletin*,
c. August 1919

A dapper Low wheels his props to a
new stage. The lay figure has not yet
assumed the habits of Lloyd George,
Neville Chamberlain, Hitler or
Mussolini, but the top hat trembles
on the brink of ridicule, and the
bottle of gall gives fair warning.

OFF TO LONDON

Confidence led him to take risks: resigning from the *Spectator*
before he had fixed a job at the *Canterbury Times*; going to the
Bulletin with only a six-month contract; most dramatically, in
his private life, cabling a proposal of marriage to a girl in New
Zealand who had turned him down already before he left for
London and whom he barely knew. (This time she accepted.)
Resourcefulness made him a good businessman, who in London
handled negotiations that might have been left to an agent; who,
as a boy, learnt to cope with cheats and people angered by his
drawings; and who, in the spirit of Tom Sawyer, laid off the cost
of his college fees by passing on the instruction to two friends
at half-rates.

As Low set out for London, then, he was the embodiment of
what may be achieved through 'learning by doing'. His technique,
cast of mind and view of the cartoonist's job were largely set.
He had a reputation across Australia and New Zealand. Now he
would win one abroad.

Low set about learning England in the same way as he learnt
Australia: by hard work and total immersion. 'Dave' Low, the
diminutive by which he continued to be known in Australia, was
about to become David. 'I never want to work so hard again
in this life,' he wrote to the *Bulletin* on his first Fleet Street anniver-

sary; '... the awful sweat and toil of having to learn up the new people and the new politics kept me so close at it'.[10]

His first British cartoon was published on 20 October 1919. Naturally there were problems settling in. He had not been used to the haste of turning out a cartoon every day, five days a week. He thought he was going to the *Daily News*, the leading metropolitan Liberal morning paper. Instead he found himself on its evening stablemate, the *Star*, tabloid in size and with a circulation of 400,000 restricted to London. Worst of all, he was expected to compete in the same mode as 'Poy' (Percy Fearon), the highly popular cartoonist of the *Star*'s larger circulation rival, Lord Northcliffe's Conservative *Evening News*. Low's individualism straightaway rebelled. Poy cartooned in a convention which, in

22 'So far, so bad!', *Lloyd George & Co.*, London, Allen & Unwin, 1921

Low juxtaposes the vote-catching promise 'Homes Fit for Heroes' with the empty reality of the Lloyd George Government's record in the immediate postwar years.

Lloyd George is pictured as a careless rogue, cocky and casual in his ability to charm without delivering. Health Minister Addison, by contrast, looks confused and unsure of himself. During his early days at the *Star*, Low made frequent use of a conventional John Bull.

SO FAR, SO BAD!

contrast with Low's ambitions, was satisfied by a smaller two-column space, cared little for draughtsmanship or printing quality, and laid no great stress on caricature. Low thumped the boardroom table: there had been a mistake; he could not do Poy's kind of work; he had to have space and be allowed to do things his own way, right down to freehand frames and lettering.

Low's self-confidence once again proved sound. He won more space, though not the full half-page he wanted. The piano-case principle lived on, for it was agreed that he could work at his studio in Hampstead; and he was given 'the status of a signed contributor responsible for his own opinions'. The Cadbury Press at this time supported the section of the Liberal Party led by Asquith, which had refused to back Lloyd George's coalition after the end of the war. One hundred and thirty-four Coalition Liberals had been returned to the Commons in the 1918 general election. But only a straggle of independent Liberals – thirty at most – rallied behind Asquith, who lost his own seat. The Labour Party, moreover, was growing and had won fifty-nine seats. Radical politics and parties were thus in flux, and Low felt comfortable enough.

Low thought the best art school was the top of a bus.[11] His boyhood hero, Phil May, had illustrated a book of lighthearted articles about the London of the 1890s, *The Parson and the Painter*. Low persuaded his editor to revive the idea. With F. W. Thomas, a gifted humorous and descriptive writer already on the *Star*, Low went sightseeing every week. As 'Low and I' they filled a page each Monday in 'not so much the spirit of humour as of boyish glee'.[12] The Zoo, Billingsgate, Hampton Court; the scope of course was endless, especially as they went out of London to holiday resorts and places such as Stratford. The series ran for years and continued with a new partner, 'Terry' (Horace Thorogood), when Low moved to the *Evening Standard* in 1927. It was also widely imitated, and it spawned two anthologies: *Low and I* (1923) and *The Low and I Holiday Book* (1925).

Learning British politics was less straightforward. But Low's experience observing parliamentarians and party movements in Australia was not altogether irrelevant, and it provided him with some introductions – to Ramsay MacDonald, for instance. Besides, many of the leading British personalities had become familiar names during the war. Low went to the Press Gallery, listened and talked, and benefited from the *Star*'s Liberal connections. Some months after he arrived, there was a by-election in Paisley, significant because Asquith was attempting (successfully)

23 'With the Boys at Billingsgate', *Low and I*, London, Methuen, 1923

'Therefore I feel bound to place it on record that the men of Billingsgate *do* swear. I have heard them. Frequently. Further than that I dare not go. There is a lot of ice about the place, and maybe they do it to keep themselves warm . . .' (F. W. Thomas, *Low and I*, pp. 36–37)

24 Bonar Law, John Simon, Ramsay MacDonald, *Star*, *c.* 1921

Column-filler sketches were an early feature of Low's work on the *Star*. Bonar Law, though yet to be Prime Minister (1922–23), was nearing the end of his career. The drawing of a youthful Sir John Simon contrasts strongly with the cartoon version familiar in the 1930s.

'Bonar in Brighter Mood'

Sir John Simon

Mr Ramsay MacDonald

25 Sketch for Asquith portrait, 1920

On a large sheet of paper, Low has placed a pensive, almost sombre Asquith at the bottom edge. It is as if the grand old man is slipping from our view. Drawn from life during the Paisley by-election, Low found Asquith '. . . aloof, old, worn, uncommunicative and more than a little crusty. . . . Asquith won. But I returned to London with the feeling of having come from overseas just in time to catch the twilight of the old prewar generation' (*Autobiography*, pp. 101–102).

to return to the Commons. Low spent ten days there and enjoyed his best opportunity yet to observe party leaders close at hand. ('Who is that young man with the eyebrows that follows me about?' enquired Asquith.)[13]

So resourceful and confident a young man was bound to find his opportunities. Whether he would *grasp* British politics so quickly was another matter. The earliest *Star* cartoons do have a certain superficiality; a tendency to reduce issues to neatly opposing views, mediated by a succession of John Bulls. But in fact, as several commentators remarked in due time, Low proved a very quick study. 'The real marvel of his career,' wrote the then editor of the *Daily News* ten years later, 'is the speed and completeness with which, fresh from the Antipodes, he mastered the intricacies of British political life.'[14]

What established Low most emphatically in Fleet Street and Westminster were the device of the two-headed Coalition Ass

26 *The Billy Book*, Sydney, Bookstall, 1918

The slim, paper-covered *The Billy Book* was an instant success and quickly sold 60,000 copies.

YOU LOST YOUR MONEY ON THIS -

WILL YOU WIN ON EITHER OF THESE

PRINTED & PUBLISHED BY THE DAILY NEWS LTD. LONDON, E.C.

27 (opposite) Election poster, *c.* 1922

The *Star* disapproved of Lloyd George's Coalition Government. Low's cartoons, with the discredited Coalition Ass prominent, translated well into electioneering leaflets and posters, which gained wide distribution throughout the country.

28 *Low and I*, London, Methuen, 1923

Low and I brought together a selection of the weekly features by Low and F. W. Thomas out and about in London.

29 Sketches for unpublished book *Zooalition*, *c.* 1921

Low never completed his plans for this book, which transmogrified Coalition Ministers
with varying degrees of spite. In the first picture, intended for a cover or frontispiece,
a leonine Lloyd George minds the turnstiles of the Coalition Zoo. In the second, he chases
balloons of hot air while an unamused Austen Chamberlain guards the bone of Toryism.

REFLECTIONS

and a distinctive cartoon version of Lloyd George. As Arnold Bennett rightly remarked in an introduction to Low's first anthology, *Lloyd George & Co* (1921), 'he has invented the image of Mr Lloyd George which in little more than a year has taken precedence over all the other images of Lloyd George'. It was a replay of Low versus Billy Hughes, except that Lloyd George was delighted rather than hostile and Low was attacking the inconsistencies of a Liberal–Conservative peacetime coalition, not the suitability of Lloyd George to lead it. Lloyd George, indeed, he found fascinating. The man was 'electric, magnetic'. He was much more satisfying to draw, too, than most of the Labour leaders and the ageing Liberals and Tories such as Asquith and Bonar Law.[15]

30 'Reflections', *Star, c.* 1920

Lloyd George of 1920, heading a Coalition Government of Conservatives and Liberals, is brought face to face with his radical past. On 30 July 1909 at Limehouse in the East End of London, he had bitterly attacked dukes, landlords, capitalists – the whole of the upper classes.

31 Unpublished sketches of Lloyd George, 1920s

'I have never bothered Mr Lloyd George to pose for me, because one could never capture his elusive personality from studying his shape sitting still in a chair . . .' (*Evening Standard*, 26 January 1931)

32 David Lloyd George, *New Statesman*, first series 1926

'I always had the greatest difficulty in making Ll. G. sinister in a cartoon. Every time I drew him, however critical the comment, I had to be careful or he would spring off the drawing-board a lovable cherubic little chap.' (*Autobiography*, p. 146)

THE MOKE'S PEDIGREE

33 'The Moke's pedigree', *Lloyd George & Co.*, London, Allen & Unwin, 1921

'After a lot of experiment, during which my table became littered with asses of various kinds, I almost absent-mindedly made what autograph collectors call a "ghost". I folded over a piece of paper upon one side of which a portion of drawing was still wet, so that the reproduction in reverse blotted itself upon the blank other side. And there, with a little adjustment of legs, was the Coalition Ass.' (*Autobiography*, p. 94)

The Ass was introduced within weeks of Low joining the *Star*, and it caught on famously. Until the Coalition fell at the end of 1922 Low used it over and over again, usually alongside Lloyd George and in an amazing variety of situations. Its flexibility as a device is analysed in Chapter II; but its popularity among readers no doubt owed something to an endearing, petlike quality shared by nearly all Low's animals. The idea came from Low's editor, James Douglas, who wrote an article criticising the Coalition as like a mule – an animal, in the words of a nineteenth-century jibe, 'without pride of ancestry or hope of posterity'.

Low's hardworking year was well worth while. By the end he had made his mark among the public, newsmen and politicians. Some of the contacts were beginning to go beyond acquaintance-

34 Unpublished H. G. Wells
sketch, *c.* 1924

'. . . He must be observed on the
move. I did most of the preliminary
study for my drawing of him while
he was playing that strenuous ball
game of his at Easton' (*Evening
Standard*, 26 January 1931). The ball
game Wells invented was notorious
among guests in his house at Easton
Glebe.

ship. In particular, he started a friendship with H. G. Wells. Wells
had been another of his childhood heroes – and kept his fascina-
tion. He was the best talker Low ever met, with Shaw second.

This process of getting to know people with a public reputation
was pushed along by another of Low's Australian expedients: the
preparation of portrait caricatures. A courteous request, backed
by the *Bulletin*'s card, had opened most doors in Australia. Why
not do the same in London? 'Listing fifty names of the most distinguished men of the time, writers, artists, scientists, photographers
. . ., I wrote to each of them expressing my wish to draw him

"Ramsay"

in the Daumier manner. I sent out the letters in batches of three as seemed opportune.'[16] Some – Wells, Ramsay MacDonald, Asquith, Lloyd George – he had already met. Kipling regretted that 'the pressure of my work and engagements does not permit me to give myself the pleasure of the interview you suggest', politely concealing an antipathy dating from Max Beerbohm's cruel caricatures of him.[17] Galsworthy also declined, but Low drew him without a sitting.

The portraits took five years to complete. The editor of the *New Statesman*, Clifford Sharp, whom Low met through the writer Robert Lynd, bought the rights to first publication of 'a dozen or more'. He also organised one or two sitters, such as the *Observer* editor J. L. Garvin ('I thought his first things were splendid,' Garvin replied).[18] In the end, Sharp published twenty, first

35 (opposite) Ramsay MacDonald, *New Statesman*, first series 1926

'I was perhaps too greatly impressed by Ramsay MacDonald, who looked to me a real leader. He seemed taller in those days and more craggy, as he stalked up and down. A handsome figure, fine voice, shabby blue serge suit, handlebar moustache solid black against solid white of hair forelock. I enjoyed drawing him' (*Autobiography*, p. 102)

Max Beerbohm's comment to a friend was: 'Ramsay MacDonald excellent: the self-made Scotsman revelling in himself and his purity and integrity and readiness and tenacity and all the rest of it . . .'

Hilaire Belloc

36 Hilaire Belloc, *New Statesman*, first series 1926

Low confessed to 'three goes' at getting Belloc right, but later thought that this likeness was 'the best portrait of that first series'. Belloc obviously agreed, for he inscribed a print 'The only true image of the writer in his age.' (*Autobiography*, p. 134)

37 Winston Churchill, *New Statesman*, first series 1926

'Winston belongs to that sandy type – as does Mr Baldwin – which cannot be rendered properly in black lines . . . Once he made me blush by advancing across a room full of people with pencil and paper, ostentatiously pretending to make a sketch of ME.' (Low, *Evening Standard*, 26 January 1931)

38 (opposite) Joseph Conrad, *New Statesman*, first series 1926

'Another job I enjoyed was Joseph Conrad. He was a beautiful dark study, with a countenance which I can only describe as suggesting an extremely kind and likeable Old Nick. He wore purple socks. When I showed him a few rough notes (I never learn caution) he looked at them in what appeared to me to be a pained silence. I remember telling him that the finished drawing would not be anything like the notes and he answered "I hope not."' (*Ye Madde Designer*, p. 85)

In the event, Conrad died in 1924, well before this caricature was published in the *New Statesman*.

as inserts to the *New Statesman*, starting in January 1926, and then singly (2/6d, framed) or in a folio (45/-). Low received a fee of eight guineas for each study and a $33\frac{1}{3}$% royalty (25% on the framed ones). He offered some of the originals for sale at about twenty guineas. The quality of offset-lithography pleased him, but he was annoyed to find that the plates wore out, as he had expected to take further copies. The publisher Jonathan Cape secured the book rights, broaching the matter through the *New Statesman* literary editor, Desmond MacCarthy. He added sixteen

Joseph Conrad
Sept. 1923

LOW

WOULD YOU MIND TAKING YOUR VICTIM A LITTLE
FURTHER ALONG, YOU'LL WAKE THE BABY...

39 & 40 'Would you mind taking your victim a little further along, you'll wake the baby . . .', *Punch*, 14 November 1923

On 3 October 1923 Frank Reynolds, art editor of *Punch*, wrote to Low: '. . . I should like to use the *you'll wake the baby* one but we do not care to use half-tone – Would it be too much to ask you to do the subject in pen? – If you should decide to do this I should suggest that you make the window higher up, more like a bedroom. Hope you agree with this.' He even provided a sketch showing how the window should be moved.

drawings not previously published, making thirty-six in all. To accompany them, in the *Vanity Fair* tradition, Cape commissioned profiles from Rebecca West. The volume appeared in the autumn of 1928 as *Lions and Lambs*, by Low with interpretations by 'Lynx'. It was a great success, not least, of course, with those portrayed. Wells (No. 1 in the *New Statesman* series) wrote: 'Low. You are really a very great man. I know my points and you have got them all.' Hilaire Belloc said the best of the bunch were understandably those of himself and of Wells. Beaverbrook thought Lloyd George and Snowden were the best 'and that of Winston is too cruel'.[19] Much innocent fun was had by reviewers guessing Lynx's identity. Harcourt Brace brought out an American edition.

Low did other work in his *Star* years, including single-column caricatures of 'Men Low Meets', a few cartoons in *Punch* and

SILENTLY THEY TRUDGED DOWN THE STEPS

41 'Silently they trudged down the slopes', *Old Seed on New Ground* by James Adderley, London, Putnam, 1920

Low conveys the motion of trudging by a diagonal design which draws the eye from figure to straggling figure, with sharply contrasting blocks of black and white.

portrait caricatures in the *Graphic*, and twelve illustrations for a book retelling the Parables in a modern setting. The author of this last, *Old Seed on New Ground*, was the popular priest Canon Jim Adderley, Rector of St. Paul's, Covent Garden, who married Low and his wife in 1920.

Low must increasingly have felt, as his reputation grew, that he could do better than the *Star*. The *Daily Herald*, for one, would have offered him a radical base, and the editor put out feelers in 1926. (Ironically, in 1919, the paper had turned down an approach from Low.)[20] Moreover, there were still periodic arguments about space. At length these proved too much. When Low's contract had come up for renewal in 1924, Lord Beaverbrook had dined and flattered him and offered to double his salary if he would join the *Evening Standard*. Low then felt disinclined. The *Standard* had not been long in Beaverbrook's hands and was dull. Perhaps

39

42 'The babe in the wood', *Star*, 4 December 1923

Two days before a general election, Low shows Baldwin, the Prime Minister, quailing before the ruffians Rothermere (*Daily Mail*) and Beaverbrook (*Daily Express*). Baldwin had called the election on the traditional issue of Protection – which he favoured – versus Free Trade, and the two press barons attacked him fiercely.

In explaining Beaverbrook's smile, Low later wrote: 'At that time his energetic personality was impressing the nation through a political booklet which carried as wrapper a photograph of the Original Beaverbrook Smile. The Smile was displayed prominently on every bookstall. So that my Beaverbrook might be more readily recognizable, therefore, my 2nd Ruffian was a smiling Ruffian . . .' (*Ye Madde Designer*, p. 95).

he felt wary too. For Beaverbrook, himself an individualist, consumed individualism in others. If Low was to continue as his own man, he would need the strongest credentials. In 1924, therefore, he stayed with a contract that continued his five cartoons a week to the *Star* (or occasionally, now, the *Daily News*) and which permitted him to do up to twelve cartoons per year in *Punch* and one caricature per week in a weekly magazine (or to hold exhibitions as an alternative), and to illustrate books and do one book a year of his own.[21]

Beaverbrook naturally continued to press: 'he shouted this offer of his at me whenever we met, regardless of whoever was present'.[22] Low cartooned him quite often, accepted such small commissions as a dinner menu from him and even discussed a project for cinema animation. He also put him in the *New States-*

Max, Lord Beaverbrook.

man series – possibly at Sharp's suggestion, for he asked for a sitting only after the series had begun. In 1927, when the *Star* contract was due for renewal again, Low was ready to deal. On 10 October his first *Evening Standard* cartoon appeared, amid the throb of a week's publicity.

It is unclear exactly how complicated were the negotiations: it suited both Low and Beaverbrook to dramatise them. The intermediary was Low's friend and fellow New Zealander F. W.

43 Max, Lord Beaverbrook, *New Statesman*, first series 1926

Lord Beaverbrook's friend and biographer, A. J. P. Taylor, wrote: 'The best likeness is the famous drawing by Low, though it makes Beaverbrook misleadingly small.' (*Beaverbrook*, London, Hamish Hamilton, 1972, p. 678).

THE HARD LOT OF A CARTOONIST.

44 'The hard lot of a cartoonist', *Evening Standard*, 13 October 1927

Whether Beaverbrook's friends had really complained about Low is immaterial. This cartoon is important because it shows Low's determination to present himself immediately on the *Evening Standard* as an independent critic. Beaverbrook, in a pose reminiscent of Low's portrait caricature, is set up as a 'straw man' along with Baldwin, Birkenhead, Churchill, Austen Chamberlain and Joynson-Hicks.

Doidge, who was connected with the *Evening Standard* management (years later he became New Zealand's Minister of External Affairs). Low does not name him in the *Autobiography*. He panders, rather, to the larger-than-life image of the press baron and describes how, arriving to sign the contract, he found Beaverbrook flat on his back behind the piano, doing exercises.[23]

The point that set the gossip running, before and after the *Evening Standard* deal was fixed, was whether Beaverbrook would really let Low express independent views. Beaverbrook was broadly Conservative: Low was radical. Neither was a party man: but that made their individuality the more precious. Each needed newspapers for a means of expression. 'I think the E.S. offers you wider possibilities than you have had before,' scribbled Clifford Sharp, '*but* – how long, oh my Lord, how long? Is it not likely to be just as long as my Lord continues to regard you as an excellent joke?'[24]

Even – perhaps especially – from a friend, such comments must

THE DIFFICULTY OF SHAKING HANDS WITH GODS.

have been unnerving. They came at Low from all sides, privately and in the press. Surely he must either go under, humiliated, or bob in the eddies of Beaverbrook's policies, carried wherever they went. Small wonder that he became 'exaggeratedly defensive'.[25]

The contract clause on which the issue would turn was, characteristically, drawn up by Low himself: '*Policy:* It is agreed that you are to have complete freedom in the selection and treatment of subject-matter for your cartoons and in the expression therein of the policies in which you believe.'[26]

The clause worked. For twenty-three years, until the 'Black Friday' in 1949 when Beaverbrook had Low's letter saying he was going to the *Daily Herald*, the *Evening Standard* was Low's base. The period was unarguably his heyday; more particularly the period up to the early years of the Second World War. The starkness of events suited the pen of a black-and-white artist. International affairs often lend themselves well to cartoon treatment, and the posturings and rhetoric of European Fascists made rich material for a radical opponent. The *Standard* was an excellent

45 'The difficulty of shaking hands with gods', *Evening Standard*, 9 November 1933

As if in a music-hall turn, Low's figures misunderstand their cues. Goebbels, Goering and Hitler, armed with the lily of innocence, distance themselves from the proffered hand of friendship. Litvinoff, Simon and Dolfuss (front) look perplexed.

The cartoon was occasioned by the withdrawal of Germany from the Geneva Disarmament Conference on 14 October 1933.

43

HOME SECRETARY
Rᵀ Hᵒⁿ EDGAR WALLACE

LABOUR
Rᵀ Hᵒⁿ AUGUSTUS JOHN

CHANCELLOR
DUCHY OF LANCASTER
Rᵀ Hᵒⁿ HANNEN SWAFFER

BOARD OF TRADE
Rᵀ Hᵒⁿ DEAN INGE

INDIA
Rᵀ Hᵒⁿ C.B.COCHRAN

COLONIES AND DOMINIONS
Rᵀ Hᵒⁿ GORDON SELFRIDGE

LORD PRESIDENT
OF THE COUNCIL
Rᵀ Hᵒⁿ EARL
OF BRIGHTON
(né HARRY PRESTON)

EDUCATION
Rᵀ Hᵒⁿ H.G.WELLS

CHANCELLOR OF
EXCHEQUER
Rᵀ Hᵒⁿ LOW
(WITH
UNDER-SECRETARY)

PRIME MINISTER
and SECRETARY FOR PEACE
Rᵀ Hᵒⁿ BERNARD SHAW

AGRICULTURE
Rᵀ Hᵒⁿ LLOYD GEORGE

FOREIGN AFFAIRS
(THIS WORLD AND THE NEXT)
Rᵀ Hᵒⁿ SIR OLIVER LODGE

LORD PRIVY SEAL
Rᵀ Hᵒⁿ BARON BABYLON
(né ARNOLD BENNETT)

THE IDEAL CABINET.

46 'The ideal cabinet', *Evening Standard*, 1 November 1928

Four writers appear with assorted commentators, critics, clergymen and a businessman in Low's 'Cabinet fit for cartoonists'. Lloyd George is the only practising politician. Lodge became well known as a spiritualist and broadcaster. Preston is pictured in the boxing scene in *The Modern Rake's Progress*. Low suggested that he compiled his list to replace the rather featureless rulers then in office with people chosen from among 'the national resources of colourful personality'.

base from which to work. Beaverbrook had acquired it when the Hulton newspaper interests were dispersed in 1923. By contrast with the *Daily Express*, which in 1936 would top two million and become the nation's best selling daily, the *Standard* was Beaverbrook's plaything. He made it progressively livelier, although its circulation, 424,000 in 1923, fell to 334,000 in 1929 and grew only spasmodically thereafter. More significantly, by 1934 the first systematic readership survey of the British press showed that it was 'very definitely the favourite evening paper of the wealthier classes of London and the South-East'.[27] About half of the 'top' twenty-five per cent of Londoners saw an evening paper. (Rather less than half of the rest did, and most of these saw the *Evening News* or *Star*.) By now, too, the old clubland evening papers such as the *Pall Mall Gazette*, with matchstick circulations in tens rather than hundreds of thousands, had disappeared. In features such as the *Standard*'s Londoner's Diary an echo of their old insider gossip murmured on. It was the right evening

(LEFT TO RIGHT)
A "FRANK" WOMAN NOVELIST, SHAKESPERE, SHAW, WELLS, BENNETT, ALDOUS HUXLEY,
D. H. LAWRENCE, JAMES JOYCE. · EACH IS ACCOMPANIED BY HIS LITERARY INSPIRATION.
(AT BACK) DICKENS AND JANE AUSTEN

JIX, THE SELF-APPOINTED CHUCKER-OUT.

paper for the thinking man's cartoonist. Low's reach, moreover, was greatly extended by syndication, which brought him a combined circulation of probably a million or more in the provinces.

The relationship with Beaverbrook was crucial. Beaverbrook's individualist politics, typified in the Empire Crusade, when he put up by-election candidates against the official Conservatives in 1930–31, acted as counterpoint to Low. Low opposed the Crusade in his cartoons, just as he opposed Beaverbrook's editorial line on Nazi Germany in the 1930s – and much else that Beaverbrook campaigned for. '. . . Brilliant in drawing, inexhaustible in invention – and, mostly, wrong in viewpoint', was Beaverbrook's comment on the anthology *Low Again* (1938).[28] So the cartoons stood out with a starkness they could not have had in a like-minded paper. The contrast was all the greater for the frequency (not truly justified by Beaverbrook's political unimportance in the rest of the 1930s) with which Low depicted his employer in the hostile cartoons.

47 'Jix, the self-appointed chucker-out', *Evening Standard*, 26 February 1929

D. H. Lawrence annotated his copy of this cartoon. To Low's caption, which reads 'Each is accompanied by his literary inspiration', Lawrence added: '. . . except me, so I suppose I've got none!' He also added his signature and the place of writing: 'Bandol, where the Pansies were born, 2 March 1929.' A typescript of Lawrence's 'Pansies', loosely based on Pascal's *Pensées*, had been seized by the police. The Home Secretary, Sir William Joynson-Hicks (Jix) subsequently stated in Parliament that he had given Lawrence two months to establish that the 'Pansies' did not contain anything indecent – but assuring the House that they did.

COL. BLIMP:
"GAD, SIR, THIS RAFT IS GETTING POSITIVELY DANGEROUS. WE SHOULD ABANDON IT AT ONCE."

S.O.S.

48 'S.O.S.', *Evening Standard*, 12 July 1935

Anthony Eden, Minister for League of Nations Affairs, and Sam Hoare, Foreign Secretary, anxiously seek support for the policy of Collective Security – increasingly precarious in the face of Italian aggression against Abyssinia. Blimp, clutching Beaverbrook's *Daily Express*, which did not support the policy anyway, proposes a characteristic alternative. Low looks alarmed.

Low, as Kingsley Martin put it after his death, 'ragged' Beaverbrook. The effect was concentrated in the Beaverbrook smile. Low admitted that Beaverbrook smiled no more than the next man. But the smile was always in the cartoons, as well as in the portrait caricature. It was a flattering image. It suggested cunning: power without entanglement – or 'without responsibility', as the Tory leader Stanley Baldwin described it in 1931, venting the frustration of the good party man. The image appealed to Beaverbrook. That was how he liked to see himself, wrote his biographer A. J. P. Taylor – the Puck or Robin Goodfellow of the political world.[29]

In fact, then, there was an essential harmony in the relationship of Beaverbrook and Low. Low's cartoons looked the stronger for being in Beaverbrook's paper and Beaverbrook could use Low to symbolise his own detachment, as newspaperman, from party ties and trammels. The two also got on well personally. Apart from mutual respect for each other's skills ('Dear Low, . . . you are the most talented man of genius', and so on), they shared the

46

THE FAVOURITES IN GOOD FORM AT ASCOT.

ENTRANCE
TO
ROYAL ENCLOSURE

HUMAN BEINGS MUST CRAWL
RESPECTFULLY ON THEIR
BREAD-BASKETS WHEN
PASSING LORD CHURCHILL,
HOLDING IN THEIR RIGHT
HANDS THEIR CERTIFICATES
OF MARRIAGE, GOOD CONDUCT
MEDALS, DISCHARGES FROM
BANKRUPTCY, TICKETS OF
LEAVE, AND BANK PASS-BOOKS

bond of being ex-colonial.[30] Not only had they 'made good', they had taken on the mother country on her own ground and triumphed. 'We both came from the outside world,' Low explained to a TV interviewer in 1959, 'and we are both without respect for institutions and persons that have no right to respect.'[31]

The contract clause 'worked' in as much as both parties publicly maintained that it worked. Like many contracts, however, it symbolised a working relationship more than actively sustaining it. Low stayed at the *Standard* because it suited him and he was never leant on too hard. Beaverbrook kept him because he never went too far – and he was good for circulation. The arrangement was little different from the Cadburys'. There, Low's contract had a clause providing that editors 'shall be at liberty at their discretion to withhold publication of any cartoon, but that no alteration shall be made to any cartoons without your approval'.[32] Beaverbrook too had a reciprocal right – which Low never emphasised and did not mention in the autobiography – to leave out cartoons. It was an agreement for mutual veto. Even so, that is not the same

49 'The favourites in good form at Ascot', unused *c.* 1938

This cartoon evidently did not suit the pages of the *Evening Standard*. Low had a predictable distaste for British snobberies. He once described the scene at Ascot as: '. . . the royal enclosure full of a sniffy mixture of persons of high moral character (official) and snobs who have wangled it, carefully fenced off from the divorcées, bankrupts, moral-perverts, burglars and other middle-class persons without social pull' (*The Best of Low*, London, Jonathan Cape, 1930, p. 209).

47

"— BUT WHAT HAVE THEY GOT IN THEIR OTHER HANDS, NANNY?"

50 '– But what have they got in their other hands, Nanny?', *Evening Standard*, 26 January 1934

Beaverbrook was embarrassed by Low's attacks on Lord Rothermere, who had helped finance his purchase of the *Evening Standard*. But Rothermere's support for Fascism was too much for Low, who softened this attack only by making the nanny unrecognisable as Rothermere and referring to the 'Daily [Black] Shirt' rather than explicitly to the *Daily Mail*.

as a requirement to draw to order; and it was this, of course, that Low would not have tolerated for a moment.

Nearly always, week in week out, Low drew what he wanted. Taylor found only two instances of Beaverbrook issuing categorical instructions. The first was in 1931, in response to pressure from Lord Rothermere. Rothermere offended easily and was Beaverbrook's ally in the Empire Crusade. More to the point, he had helped finance the purchase of the *Evening Standard*. In 1931 he still controlled forty-nine per cent of the shares and Beaverbrook was trying to buy him out. It was no time for pussy-footing if Low was making things difficult. By the time Low was attacking Rothermere again, for throwing the *Daily Mail* behind Oswald Mosley's British Union of Fascists in 1934, the shares were bought. Beaverbrook's staff cautioned Low, but Low stood his ground and they did not persist.[33]

The second case was in May 1940. The Foreign Office received an official Spanish protest about a Low cartoon attacking Franco. The Foreign Secretary, Halifax, wrote – in mild terms – to Beaverbrook ('I am sure it would be very helpful . . .'). This,

48

THE HARMONY BOYS

MUSSO'S PRESS

FRANCO'S PA[...]

PRO-NAZI PROPAGAND[A]

again, was hardly the moment to be driving Franco into the German camp, and Low desisted.[34]

A third case is quoted by Low himself: 'a spirited effort about the situation in Greece in 1945 which was blocked at the request of Churchill the Prime Minister in what he held to be the interests of Western democracy.'[35]

These were the plain examples. Low estimated that about a couple of dozen were left out from causes that, in the context of the contract clause, were innocent (the sudden illness of a person cartooned, for instance). Buckingham Palace let it be known that we do not put royalty in cartoons. Most such pressure, from home and abroad and from people of any political colour or none, Beaverbrook turned aside. Despite this, there was a trickle of cartoons omitted as a result of decisions by editors rather than by Beaverbrook himself. This might be on the advice of libel lawyers (with which Low tended to be impatient; he never cost the paper a penny in damages). Sometimes the pressure was simply a tactful request: 'we do not want at the present time to run what will seem to be a cartoonist's campaign against the dictators. You dealt

51 'The harmony boys', *Evening Standard*, 2 May 1940

One of Low's most successful compositions – which produced a Spanish Government complaint to the Foreign Office. Low points to the hand of Hitler coordinating 'official' statements from Italy, Spain and the USSR, none of whom was yet in the war.

49

THE JAW IS THE JAW OF MUSSO, BUT——

52 'The jaw is the jaw of Musso, but –', unused, c. 24 November 1936

On 24 November 1936, Percy Cudlipp, editor of the *Evening Standard*, wrote to Low: 'We have talked over the ventriloquist cartoon very carefully, and have decided to hold it over for the present for this reason: we do not want at the present time to run what will seem to be a cartoonist's campaign against the dictators . . . I suggest, therefore, that for the present you avoid the dictators altogether. Meanwhile, I should like to keep the ventriloquist cartoon by me until the present tension relaxes . . .' The 'present tension' was the Spanish Civil War.

with them on Monday . . . But a succession of such cartoons at this time might very well do serious harm . . . I suggest, therefore, that for the present you avoid the dictators altogether.'[36]

Usually Low complied. For example, an occasional cartoon strip about 'Hit and Muss' was collapsed into an identikit dictator – 'Muzzler'; and Low did from time to time adapt his choice of subject. Sometimes, however, he did not. Stanley Tiquet, deputy to the editor Percy Cudlipp, 'reminded' Low that nothing in the *Standard* should prejudice international peace and good relations during the Berlin Olympics in 1936. Low wrote on the letter: '!!? To hell with Tiquet.'[37]

The total of all such documented examples is very small. Self-censorship can of course be stricter than direct censorship. But the important point is that Low had all the latitude he normally needed from the last proprietor of whom it might have been expected – and in a press system that was only now emerging from a tradition of political partisanship where editors (never mind cartoonists) danced to the tune or went to the wall.

50

EASTER EGG SITUATION

According to Low's Office Hen, it's a bad season. Judging by the political comment from the more Blimpish West-end clubs there are a lot of wooden eggs about this year.

Care is being taken to guard Musso from 'flu in these important times. Well, that's where the Democracies can teach him something.

EASTER RABBIT CRISIS

Here, too, dissatisfaction. Rabbits are particularly sore at the way their burrows have been crowded out by city financiers.

FÜHRER TO BE KEPT IN BULLET-PROOF BOTTLE

Something must be done to protect him from his affectionate people, obviously.

THIS WEEK'S TRUE ANIMAL STORY

A dog bit Hitler. The dog went mad.

A happy holiday was spent by the High Priests, exorcising demons from the Labour Party. Soon we'll have all the clever ones out and the awful danger of getting into power during the next 100 years will be avoided.

BLACK MAGIC AT TRANSPORT HOUSE

· **53** Low's Topical Budget, unused, n.d.

'A dog bit Hitler. The dog went mad.' This was too strong a joke for the sensitivities of Low's bosses. So was the jibe at an embottled Hitler. As the initials 'HO' (Hold Over) indicate, this Topical Budget was not used.

HIT AND MUSS ON THEIR AXIS OUR COMIC STRIP

HIT AND MUSS ON THEIR AXIS. OUR COMIC STRIP

54 'Hit and Muss on their axis', *Evening Standard*, 6 and 13 November 1937

The *Evening Standard*'s editor, Percy Cudlipp, had turned down the 'Hit and Muss' idea less than two months earlier: 'I have been thinking over your "Hit and Muss" idea and I would prefer that you did not do this just now' (17 September 1937). Previously he had pointed to some of the difficulties then faced by editors:

'. . . The state of Europe is extremely tense at the present time. That being so, I don't want to publish anything in the "Evening Standard" which would add to the tension, or inflame tempers any more than they are already inflamed. There are people whose tempers are inflamed more by a cartoon than by any letterpress. So will you please, when you are planning your cartoons, bear in mind my anxiety on this score?' (9 September 1937).

55 (opposite) 'Muzzler', *Evening Standard*, 1 and 8 January 1938

Low's response to Cudlipp's anxiety was to combine Hit and Muss into an identikit dictator, 'Muzzler' – a typical Low pun.

PERSONAL EXPLANATION DEPT.

Certain sensitive persons, under the impression (profoundly mistaken, of course) that our comic strip HIT AND MUSS referred to themselves, threaten World War if it be continued. In the sacred cause of Peace, therefore, this BUDGET makes the Supreme Sacrifice.

In future this corner will be occupied by

LOW'S OWN PRIVATE DICTATOR
MUZZLER

POSITIVELY NO CONNECTION WITH ANY OTHER ESTABLISHMENT

Complaints dealt with in rotation

MUZZLER WITH CHILD AND BEERPOT AT CHRISTMAS, SHOWING THAT HE IS JUST A BIG-HEARTED BOY

MUZZLER   *DARING ATTEMPT ON LIFE OF OUR DICTATOR*

Borne from Olympia through Greece by a Greek athlete

the torch will be carried through Bulgaria by King Boris,

through Jugoslavia by Peter the Boy King,

OLYMPIC TORCH TOUR

thence to Germany, where Hitler will probably forget himself and set fire to some inoffensive Jew

CONCENTRATION CAMP FOR CHAMPS

Hitler, who wanted the Olympic Games to sweeten relations between Nazi Germany and Britain, is said to be peeved with German athletes who so far forgot themselves as to win. Disciplinary measures are likely.

56 'Olympic torch tour', *Evening Standard*, 25 July 1936 and 'Concentration camp for champs', *Evening Standard*, 8 August 1936 (Low's Topical Budget, extracts)

Hitler planned to use the Berlin Olympic Games as propaganda for Nazi Germany. But Low saw them as another opportunity to attack the regime – and ignored editorial requests to go easy.

Low had a guaranteed half-page for his cartoon in the *Evening Standard*, four days a week. He was pleased too by the quality of block-making and printing. He always paid great attention to technical matters. At least one paper was dropped from his syndication list in Canada after the Second World War because of its poor printing.

Low's working routine continued on modified piano-case lines. He never worked in the office, nor even at home until the Blitz. He had a studio in Hampstead (13a Heath Street) – minus telephone, and no callers – some thirty minutes' walk away. 'I wake at 8 o'clock and read the newspapers until about half-past nine,' he told an interviewer in 1935. '. . . Then by half-past ten, after breakfast and perhaps a game of tennis, I'm walking across Hampstead Heath to my studio. It's in the course of that walk that I get my ideas. I get to the studio about eleven and by a quarter-past I am at work. If ideas are coming they are pinned down by one o'clock. Then the actual drawing begins. The time that this takes depends, of course, upon the number of figures. Sometimes it takes two hours, sometimes more. I am not a quick worker; and I have no great admiration for quick work.' The cartoon was collected by a messenger.[38]

The routine varied, of course. Low liked to try out ideas over the breakfast table with his wife and, as they grew up, with his two daughters. The games changed: his curiosity, and avowed incompetence, made him experiment – with archery, for instance.

57 Low at work in his studio at 13a Heath Street, Hampstead, *Picture Post*, 22 October 1938

The day's idea might come earlier or later. When he was older, he found things crystallised best in the morning bath. The rough draft might take more or less time to refine. Many cups of tea were necessary: he used to joke that he needed thirteen or fourteen a day. Props, including a long mirror, were essential. In Australia, he liked to tell, the town hall once sent round a steam-roller for him. He drew with a brush over a pencil sketch, a technique he adopted in Australia. Tomorrow's cartoon was done today, for an evening paper. But increasing syndication no doubt made him have to think further and further ahead. A habit which started in the early 1930s was of relaxing for an hour in a cinema most evenings before dinner. (There were three within ten minutes' walk.) 'I don't take much notice of the story of the films . . . I enjoy my cigar and just abandon myself to the pictures.'[39]

Low was showered with ideas for cartoons, from friends and the famous as well as from ordinary readers. The letters from the famous now sound the more embarrassing for their bashfulness. J. M. Barrie, Aldous Huxley, Leonard Woolf, Howard Spring, the Bishop of Chichester and the Master of Downing College, Cambridge: they and many others laboriously put their happy visual ideas into words. During the war Herbert Morrison even suggested a cartoon about a speech he was going to make in a few days' time. Low found the ideas unusable. Illustrated jokes and a collaborative tradition on the *Bulletin* had been one thing; the work of an independent Fleet Street political cartoonist was another. Most of the ideas were unoriginal. Some were unpractical: 'Writers cannot usually be of much help to artists, for makers of words and makers of pictures don't think along the same lines.'[40] The greater his reputation, moreover, the more likely might a 'contributor' expect payment or copyright. Ideas were, in any case, no problem for Low. Selection and refinement were the difficult part.

This routine applied primarily to the core of Low's work: the four cartoons for the *Evening Standard*. He did fewer casual drawings than he had for the *Star*. His dog 'Musso' had illustrated a regular weather report and he had drawn the occasional poster and full-page advertisement for the *Star*'s free insurance scheme (a staple of newspaper competition in those days). Apart from continuing the 'Low and I' format with 'Low and Terry', which he found a welcome change from the pressure of foreign affairs in the 1930s, his main innovation was the Saturday 'Topical Budget'. This appeared first on 21 April 1934 billed as 'a full page of humorous drawings reviewing current events', and it ceased,

58 (above and opposite) 'At the waxworks', *Low and Terry*, London, Hutchinson, 1934

'When Low heard I had never been to Madame Tussaud's he was astonished. He couldn't understand it. He said, did my parents ill-treat me in any other way?...' (*Low and Terry* [Horace Thorogood], p. 200)

59 (opposite) Low's Topical
Budget, *Evening Standard*, 9 June 1934

Political allusions mix with social
comment in an early Topical Budget.
The zoo provides a pretext for
poking fun at Ramsay MacDonald
(the Prime Peanut) and J. H.
Thomas, while Low's dog Musso
writes 'art criticism' about
calisthenics in the park. The bottom
panel draws attention to an
experimental form of pedestrian
crossing – forerunner of the 'Belisha
Beacon' and zebra crossing.

60 (following page) *Bulletin*, 27
August 1914

This cartoon shows both the
Australian origins of Low's Topical
Budget and the forerunners of
Colonel Blimp. The fat man on the
weighing machine, with young Low
in attendance, could almost be Blimp
– but for his lack of self-contradiction
or inconsistency. He is Blimp with an
immature Australian accent.

61 (following page) Low's Topical
Budget, *Evening Standard*, 9 October
1937

Three years after its introduction, the
Topical Budget formula remains the
same. This reproduction from the
original shows an amendment to
Low's text in the bottom left corner.

only as a result of paper shortages, on 16 March 1940. Apart from
the pleasing echo of Low's *Big Budget* debut in its name, the feature
had Australian roots, in that Low was experienced in filling a
weekly page of cartoons. The Topical Budgets became a kind
of combination of the frivolous social comment in 'Low and I'
with the pointed thrusts of the political cartoons. They included
a number of recurring characters, easily the most notable being
Colonel Blimp. The page was designed with enormous skill.
When it was left out one day in 1938, from what Low regarded
as groundless fears of libel, he angrily told the editor that 'it drains
me more than two cartoons', and threatened to stop drawing it
altogether.[41]

The Topical Budgets, like the regular cartoons, were syndicated
to a dozen or more evening papers in important centres such as
Glasgow, Birmingham, Manchester and Newcastle. For reasons
of competition, the syndication to morning papers was limited
to the *Manchester Guardian* which started taking the cartoons in
1931.

Abroad, the cartoons circulated widely in the Empire – especially, for obvious reasons, in Australia and New Zealand. In the
USA distribution took time to build up. Individual cartoons were
occasionally reproduced, as were some of the *New Statesman* caricatures. In 1928 a Low cartoon had the distinction of being the
first ever sent across the Atlantic by wireless. The agent used by
the *Evening Standard*, E. B. Dancy, built up a list of about twenty-
five papers in 1932–33, which received blocks from Canada by
air. But after losing money he restricted himself to an arrangement
with the *New York Times*. At the end of 1936, Beaverbrook's own
syndication service took over and handled Low all round the
world for the rest of his career, including the many requests for
'one-off' reproductions. The *New York Times* continued to publish him in the Sunday edition; and it occasionally permitted
repeat publication in about ten other papers such as the *St. Louis
Post-Despatch*. Cartoons appeared also in the weekly *Nation*. After
the war, the *New York Times* connection ended. A Canadian
syndicate secured the newspaper rights and sold Low's work, with
that of Strube and Giles, to 'a select list of dailies' such as the *New
York Herald Tribune* and the *Boston Globe*, as well as to twenty-five
Canadian dailies. *Time-Life* took the magazine rights, with the
Nation.[42] Low always tended to be much more concerned with
the quality of reproduction (faint lines easily got lost, spoiling
a caricature; captions could be tampered with) than with max-
imising the number of outlets.

LOW'S TOPICAL BUDGET

REFLECTIONS ABOUT WAR, BY A SYDNEY ARTIST

LOW's TOPICAL BUDGET

PASSING OF "DEAR-OLD-LEICESTER-SQ." SOB-STUFF

"Fer Heaven's sake dry up, 'Arry. You're breaking my 'eart."

MEM'RIES OF ALHAMBRA

DALY'S

RELIEF OF BOURNEMOUTH
TOWN NOW FREE FROM RED TERROR

SURVIVORS EMERGE FROM GAS-PROOF SHELTERS UPON RETREAT OF LABOUR CONFERENCE

A STAR IS BORN

A B C

Shooting of the epic which is to swell the Prime Minister's film fan following is held up for the moment. Mr. Korda, studying his poissonality, is undecided whether to make him up as a Robert Taylor type (EXHIBIT A), a Jack Hulbert sort of fellow (B) or something glamorous and exotic like Merle Oberon (C).

STOP PRESS LATEST.—Definitely Groucho Marx official.

Park-lovers are delighted now that enclosures have been provided big enough to dump not only litter but also litterers.

NO EARLY MORNING FITNESS BROADCAST

Despite all the B.B.C.'s specious excuses Low knows the real reason, the big lazybones.

Gad, sir, Mussolini is right. It's high time the Japanese War Office reprimanded the Archbishop of Canterbury for his unchristian conduct.

MORRIS DANCE

Special Motor Show attraction. Tableau of the famous philanthropist, Lord Nuffield, pursued by a subscription-hunter in one of the fast cars produced by the famous motor manufacturer, Lord Nuffield.

GIDDAP! BY COL. BLIMP

LOW's TOPICAL BUDGET

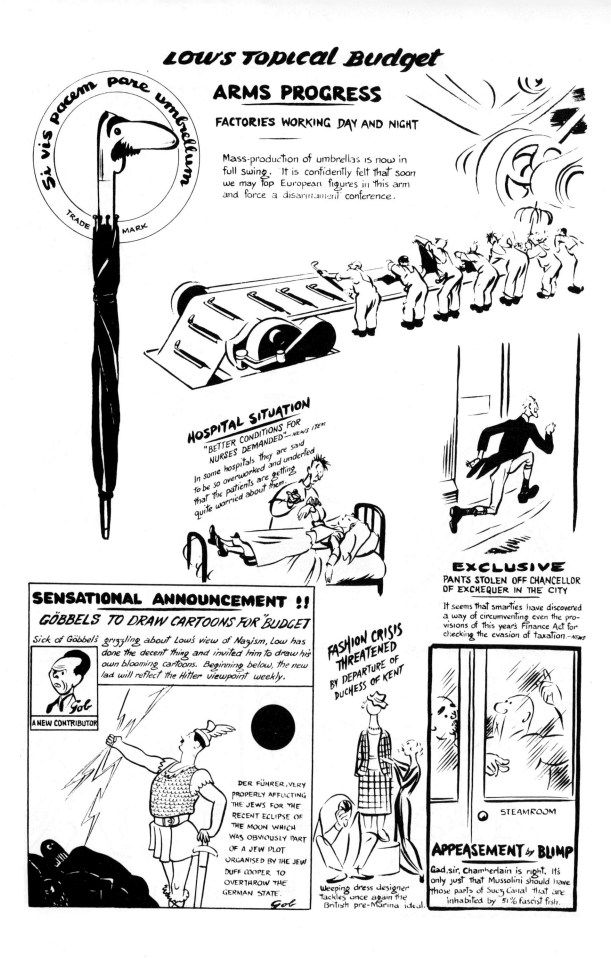

ARMS PROGRESS

FACTORIES WORKING DAY AND NIGHT

Mass-production of umbrellas is now in full swing. It is confidently felt that soon we may top European figures in this arm and force a disarmament conference.

Si vis pacem pare umbrellum

TRADE MARK

HOSPITAL SITUATION

"BETTER CONDITIONS FOR NURSES DEMANDED" — NEWS ITEM

In some hospitals they are said to be so overworked and underfed that the patients are getting quite worried about them.

EXCLUSIVE

PANTS STOLEN OFF CHANCELLOR OF EXCHEQUER IN THE CITY

It seems that smarties have discovered a way of circumventing even the provisions of this year's Finance Act for checking the evasion of taxation. — NEWS

SENSATIONAL ANNOUNCEMENT !!

GÖBBELS TO DRAW CARTOONS FOR "BUDGET"

Sick of Göbbels' grizzling about Low's view of Nazism, Low has done the decent thing and invited him to draw his own blooming cartoons. Beginning below, the new lad will reflect the Hitler viewpoint weekly.

A NEW CONTRIBUTOR

Göb

DER FÜHRER, VERY PROPERLY AFFLICTING THE JEWS FOR THE RECENT ECLIPSE OF THE MOON WHICH WAS OBVIOUSLY PART OF A JEW PLOT ORGANISED BY THE JEW DUFF COOPER TO OVERTHROW THE GERMAN STATE.

Göb

FASHION CRISIS THREATENED

BY DEPARTURE OF DUCHESS OF KENT

Weeping dress designer tackles once again the British pre-Marina ideal.

STEAMROOM

APPEASEMENT by BLIMP

Gad, sir, Chamberlain is right. It's only just that Mussolini should have those parts of Suez Canal that are inhabited by 51% fascist fish.

With the rise of international tension in Europe, Low's graphic comment attracted much interest in the USA, especially after he visited there in the Autumn of 1936. He started contributing occasional articles to the *New York Times* magazine, a practice which continued until after the war. A series of cartoons for the illustrated British news magazine, *Picture Post*, starting in October 1939, were also wired to the American *Collier's*. In 1938 he contributed about a dozen cartoons to a new American offshoot of *Esquire*, a fortnightly called *Ken*. The deal was arranged by cable. 'Your Politics Fit Ken Like Glove,' the editor wired. Low agreed to do six drawings initially, at $200 each (then worth about £40). (They offered $150 at first.) The *Standard* had no objection, as the magazine would not be circulating in Britain. The subject matter, cabled again, was 'Your Impression Present and Coming Muddle World Affairs'.

62 (opposite) Low's Topical Budget, *Evening Standard*, 12 November 1938

Neville Chamberlain's umbrella became such a hallmark that Low here fuses it with Chamberlain himself, simultaneously making a neat point about Britain's lack of armaments. The Latin motto is a pun on the tag, *Si vis pacem, para bellum* – 'If you want peace, prepare for war.' (Low has misspelt *para*. For his autobiography, he redrew the motto correctly.) In other panels, Low takes a dig at Sir John Simon (Chancellor of the Exchequer) and at Dr Goebbels; pays an indirect compliment to Princess Marina, Duchess of Kent, as a leader of fashion; and makes a characteristic joke by reversing the roles of patients and nurses. Blimp is his usual self in his usual place.

'IT'

63 'It', *Star*, 18 August 1925

Hobbs, the hero of England's cricket team, had 'it' – that indefinable extra something – at a time when the 'it' girl, filmstar Clara Bow, was all the rage. Harmless enough at home, the depiction of Mahomet meant that in India the cartoon 'convulsed many Moslems in speechless rage', as the Calcutta correspondent of the *Morning Post* put it. Meetings were held and resolutions of protest were passed.

FOLLOW MY LEADER

64 'Follow my leader', *Ken, c.* 1938

One of a series in 1938 for the American magazine *Ken*. The generalised subject reflects the difficulties of long-distance cartooning. Low had to draw a whole month ahead of publication. Hitler was apt to move faster.

Ken was pleased with the cartoons, but Low felt that 'my overloaded camel must have a few bales of straw taken off his hump'. He ended the connection after six months. A surprising side-effect was a possible libel case. The Conservative MP and former Beaverbrook editor, Beverley Baxter (like Beaverbrook, a Canadian), wrote a newspaper article ('Those Who Slander Britain') attacking the *Ken* cartoons as treacherous. Egged on by Kingsley Martin, editor of the *New Statesman*, of which Low was now a director, Low took legal advice. 'If the lawyers think you have a good case, I'd like you to bung in a writ,' wrote Martin, 'as I am keen on people of our kind making good use of the libel racket while the going's good.' Counsel's advice was that Low had good grounds for an action but might be unwise on non-legal grounds to bring it: a political cartoonist 'must be prepared to stand for a lot'. The experience gained Low nothing and lost him time and the lawyers' fee. He does not appear to have contemplated legal action against a critic on any other occasion.[43]

DO STUFFED ANIMALS MAKE GOOD GIFTS FOR NERVOUS CHILDREN ?

Low did a variety of work outside the press. *The Best of Low* (1930) was an anthology of 101 of the *Standard* cartoons, with quite detailed annotations. Reviews were good, but Low seems to have been a reluctant anthologist until the late 1930s (unlike his *Daily Express* counterpart Strube, who used to produce an annual). Perhaps he was cautious of devaluing the currency. *Low's Political Parade* did not appear until 1936, and the air of anthology was slightly reduced by the chronological disordering of the cartoons. By now Blimp was in full flow – as were the Dictators and Low's attacks. The book was a bestseller. The Communist *Daily Worker*'s reviewer, its cartoonist Gabriel, delighted in drawing attention to the inclusion of two cartoons not previously published. The reason, he implied, was their unacceptability to the Beaverbrook proprietorship. One of them was a sympathetic view of the Russian Five-Year Plan; the other, a criticism of the international banking system during the 1931 crash. Low referred to their non-publication in his introduction but gave no explanation. *Low Again* appeared in identical format and with comparable success in 1938.

65 'Do stuffed animals make good gifts for nervous children?', *Evening Standard*, 8 December 1927

Low links his mistrust of the nationalism on display at the Geneva Disarmament Conference to a pre-Christmas boom in stuffed toys. Stresemann, Mussolini, Austen Chamberlain, Briand and Coolidge are the villains. Low's composition gives a strong sense of movement, crowding the little girl. He pokes fun, too, at such traditional national symbols as the lion and eagle.

MICKY MOUSE SEEKS PROTECTION.

66 'Micky Mouse seeks protection', *Evening Standard*, 28 February 1934

Austria became a test of strength between Hitler and Mussolini in 1934. Chancellor Dollfuss was Mussolini's puppet, and when Nazis murdered him Mussolini responded with troops to the Brenner Pass.

The depiction of Dollfuss owes a lot to the Disney cartoon character Mickey Mouse (misspelt by Low).

Reviewers were beginning to describe Low as 'a national institution'. His growing international audience was reflected in the publication of *A Cartoon History of Our Times* (1939), a special anthology for the United States with text by the well-known journalist Quincy Howe. Hitherto, English editions had been exported.

The success of *Lions and Lambs* prompted a second series of twelve *New Statesman* caricatures in 1933. More than before, it was no doubt a mark of distinction to be included. Even so, there was some jockeying of the subjects between announcement and publication, and at least one did not at that time materialise. Bertrand Russell was 'honoured by your desire to include him' – but only if Low would journey to Portmeirion in Wales for a sitting.[44] Low presumably did not, as no Russell appeared until after the war. Low sold some of the originals at an exhibition

CAUSE PRECEDES EFFECT

of his work in 1937. The one of Einstein went to Victor (later the third Baron) Rothschild for fifty guineas. Sales of *Evening Standard* cartoon originals at twenty-five guineas were less successful.

Low's friendship with Wells led to collaboration. 'Dear Low', came a letter dated 25 June 1929, in Wells' tiny script. 'I've written a silly topical novel that amuses me. It is about a Dictator in London and what happened. I suddenly saw it illustrated by you. That I suppose is impossible. But would you like to read a nice clean typescript of it?' It was not impossible at all. Low probably leapt at the chance. He did ten double-page illustrations, serialised initially in *Nash's Magazine*. Wells was delighted with them. The story itself, *The Autocracy of Mr Parham* (1930), was a political satire on the totalitarian tendencies of the time. Mr Parham is an Oxford don taken up by the wealthy and influential, including a tycoon on Beaverbrook lines and a militarist named General Gerson. A spiritualist seance gives Parham the powers to make himself Lord Paramount of England, at the head of the Duty Paramount League. The House of Commons is dismissed in Cromwellian style. A triumphant progress among the dictators of Europe,

67 'Cause precedes effect', *Evening Standard*, 20 March 1935

In January 1935 Sir John Simon felt that '. . . the practical choice is between a Germany which continues to rearm without any regulation or agreement, and a Germany which, through getting a recognition of its rights and some modifications of the peace treaties, enters into the comity of nations' (letter to George V, quoted in Harold Nicolson, *King George V*, London, Constable, 1952, p. 522).

Low is incensed that Hitler has taken advantage of the diplomatic protocol observed by other European nations. Low underlines the weakness of Simon's position by giving the Foreign Secretary jelly legs. In the front ranks march the architects of the Versailles Treaty, frequently regarded as a major cause of the eventual rise of Hitler.

68   Stanley Baldwin, *New Statesman*, second series 1933

'. . . the one I like best is Stanley
Baldwin . . . One dark night I shall
burgle the British Museum, which
has the original, and steal it back.'

(Low, *New York Times*, 2 April 1961)
    Baldwin himself was probably less
enthusiastic. He once told Arthur
Christiansen, editor of the *Daily*

Express, 'Now Low is a genius, but he is
evil and malicious. I cannot bear Low'
(Christiansen, *Headlines All My Life*,
London, Heinemann, 1961, p. 155).

Professor Einstein

Low

69   Professor Einstein, *New Statesman*, second series 1933

'I draw Professor Einstein ambling in mid-air, separate by some distance from his own shadow, a reflection upon personal relativity . . . "But that isn't like me," says an individual who has just been caricatured. "That, sir," says the caricaturist with profound truth "is more like you than you are."' (*Ye Madde Designer*, pp. 55–56)

70 *The Autocracy of Mr Parham* by
H. G. Wells (assisted by David Low),
London, Heinemann, 1930

'"Mr. Speaker," he said, "I must ask
you to leave the chair." He turned
half-face to the government benches.
"Gentlemen, the Ministers of the
Crown, I would advise you to yield
your portfolios without demur to my
secretaries. For the good of His
Majesty's realm and the needs of our
mighty Empire I must for a time take
these things over from you. When
England has found her soul again,
when her health has been restored,
then all her ancient liberties of speech
and counsel will return to her
again."' (pp. 162–63)

The benches are crowded with
recognisable politicians, including
Ramsay MacDonald, Oswald
Mosley, Stanley Baldwin and
Winston Churchill.

such as 'Paramuzzi' of Italy, culminates in the Second World War
against the Americans and the destruction of London.

There was speculation in the press about the models for the
chief characters. To prevent the possibility of libel actions, Wells
ended by pooh-poohing his own creations. Low's drawings were
none the less suggestive. The Beaverbrook is unmistakable; also
Lord Castlerosse, well known as a gossip columnist. Wells' intentions, of course, had been plain in his instructions to Low: 'Gerson? . . . A touch of Lord Byng whom I have always regarded
as the typical military fool', and so on. Low disliked having to
tone down the drawings, but he thought the project 'a lark, even
if it did not quite come off'.[45] A new novel by Wells was a
publishing event, so it was reviewed with a prominence and
enthusiasm that now look undeserved. Wells was right to call it
a silly topical novel. There are passages of fine writing, and the
story rattles along. But it is a curiosity, interesting chiefly for
Low's contributions, which at the time were noticed somewhat
in parenthesis.

Ten years later Peter Fleming wrote *The Flying Visit*, a shorter

and less grandiose fantasy that lent itself similarly to illustration by a cartoonist. Writing in March 1940 during the Phoney War and a bout of measles, Fleming played the game of 'Let's pretend'. Suppose Hitler, flying on a sortie over England for the experience, was forced to parachute down. Fleming subjects him to humiliation by the unflappable rural English, who refuse to accept that he is really the Führer. Nonplussed about what to do, the Government eventually decides that the best thing is to parachute him home again. Fleming was a gifted light writer and Low produced some characteristic Hitlers and Churchills. By an extraordinary irony Hitler's deputy Hess really did parachute into Britain months later, in May 1941, from motives that never became entirely clear. Only he was not sent home.

A different kind of collaboration was *Low's Russian Sketchbook* (1932). The title is worth noting. It could as well have been 'Kingsley Martin's Russian Diary'. E. M. Forster, reviewing it in

71 *The Flying Visit* by Peter Fleming, London, Jonathan Cape, 1940

'It was a small, shallow horse-pond. William the Conqueror, stepping for the first time onto British soil, stumbled and took seisin of it with his hand. Adolf Hitler, by landing on his rump in the mud, made an interesting and characteristic variation in the etiquette for conquistadors.' (p. 34)

'A loathsome little mongrel, in which chow predominated, came bounding out of the wood, made for Hitler from behind yapping venomously, and buried its teeth in his flying boot.' (pp. 61–62)

71

TROUBLES OF A TRACTOR INSTRUCTOR.
THE AWKWARD SQUAD.

"GOING ON THE BUST" IN RUSSIA.

Worker, just promoted, takes home the customary present for the wife.

low

RUSSIAN COUPLE DISCUSSING BIOLOGICAL UNION IN ITS RELATION TO ECONOMIC EXPEDIENCY.

low

PEASANT GOING FOR A WEEK-END Wondering if he has forgotten anything

low

the *Listener*, referred to it indeed as 'Kingsley Martin's book'. But Low's name was much the greater draw. He and Martin were among British journalists on a party invited to visit Soviet Russia in 1932. They were anxious to be fair but not gullible and to avoid the extremes of hostility or assertiveness typical of many visitors. Low's fifty-six drawings are full of his natural good humour, but the shrewd choice of subjects and captions makes them ironic to a point just short of cynicism, especially as his Russians nearly all have a wondering innocence. 'The camera may have a certain verisimilitude,' wrote the *Manchester Guardian*'s reviewer, 'but this is truth itself.'[46]

Kingsley Martin's text received more mixed reviews. Maynard Keynes, writing in Martin's own *New Statesman*, found it, gently,

72 (opposite) 'Troubles of a tractor instructor, the Awkward Squad', *Low's Russian Sketchbook*, London, Gollancz, 1932

'We were told two years ago that every tractor was smashed up on the farms as soon as it got there. But now you can see the peasants handling them quite successfully, and the Russians are turning them out quite fast now in their own factories at Stalingrad and Kharkov. And by now there must be a lot of Russian mechanics coming along . . .' (Kingsley Martin, *Low's Russian Sketchbook*, p. 105). In hindsight, Low's drawing seems much the more perceptive comment.

73 Montage of smaller drawings, *Low's Russian Sketchbook*, London, Gollancz, 1932

In addition to full-page drawings, *Low's Russian Sketchbook* is full of these smaller vignettes.

'a little too full of good will. When a doubt arises, it is swallowed down if possible'. Martin reflected in his memoirs in 1968 that 'the net effect was certainly too favourable', chiefly through over-optimism about the pace of Soviet development.[47] Now the text seems absurdly heavy and self-conscious, very much the 'schoolmaster-on-holiday account' for which the *Times Literary Supplement* criticised it in 1933.

On his return (bearded, for the first time), Low wrote a lively full-page article of impressions for the *Evening Standard*. His drawings had nearly been confiscated by a border guard, which made a good story.

Low also found time to write about the art of cartoon and caricature. The awkwardly titled *Ye Madde Designer* (how to pronounce it in bookshop or library?) appeared in 1935 after several years in the planning and a trial as three broadcast talks. Its four chapters are a mixture of analysis – especially of the relation between cartoon and caricature – anecdotes about Low's method and the people he had drawn, and potted history. The style is brisk and conversational and the anecdotal sections in particular reveal something of the art that conceals art. *British Cartoonists, Caricaturists and Comic Artists* (1942) appeared in Collins' well-known 'Britain in Pictures' series. It was an essay of some 15,000 words, highly selective, full of inevitable off-the-cuff judgements. 'One cannot help feeling,' Osbert Lancaster wrote in the *Observer*, 'that for Mr Low the history of British comic art appears as a glorious progress onwards and upwards from Hogarth to page two of the *Evening Standard*.'[48] What to say about himself had obviously been a problem. Low solved it by saying only that opinions differed and that the attitudes and intentions of his cartoons could be guessed from his comments in the book.

However hard Low worked – and he always retained a tendency to overwork – he could not fit everything in. An idea for satirical illustrations to short extracts from Hitler's *Mein Kampf* came to nothing, though Low did some tantalising rough sketches. Other projects never even got onto the drawing board. H. G. Wells dreamt up a misty idea for collaboration on a kind of 'revue-comic-opera' for which Low would do designs. During the war, they also discussed producing a set of posters and booklets on the Rights of Man, text by Wells, drawings by Low. A. A. Milne discussed a joint book too: this one would in some way have sought to 'stop the drift to war'.[49]

Most tantalising was an abandoned collaboration in 1928–29 with the historian Philip Guedalla. The idea, thought up by their

LOW'S "NASTIES".

75 'Low's "Nasties"', *Evening Standard*, 4 April 1933

Low often 'talked' to the reader in his cartoons. Here he fits 170 words into the frame; the cartoon is really an illustrated story. The sequence is beautifully composed, with the figure of Low himself – uncharacteristically fierce, and yet absurd – dominating the design.

mutual friend Robert Lynd, was for a series of essays by Guedalla upon historical figures, with caricatures by Low. Low called it 'Monumental Persons of the Past'. Correspondence continued over several months, with Low making the running – not least because Guedalla was busy as a Liberal candidate in the 1929 general election. They should leave out people 'whose appearance is purely conjectural,' suggested Guedalla, ' – this would bar Attila and your cherished Cheops.' Both the latter had been on a list of fifteen discussed between Low and Victor Gollancz, a possible publisher. The list included Caesar, Shakespeare, Nero, Cromwell, Leonardo – a thoroughly mixed bunch. Guedalla did not like Nero and Raleigh either, as they had made 'no real contribution to human achievement'. He preferred Socrates ('we must have a Greek'), Dante and Voltaire. The game could be played interminably. That it was not carried through seems partly due to general business (Guedalla was enormously busy), partly to Guedalla's hesitation about Gollancz (he felt too loyal to Hodders, his usual publisher), and partly to the difficulties of finding an

THE RAKE LEARNS OF THE INHERITANCE.
Visit of the Personal Press

76 Sketch for *The Modern Rake's Progress*, unpublished, *c.* 1934

This sketch for plate 1 of the book with Rebecca West may have been produced as a guide for the author of the text and the publisher, rather than as a working drawing. Low's usual method of constructing a work was a more methodical build-up of purposeful lines, but here he allows his pen to doodle a little. Colour is merely suggested with different inks; the line is finer, looser, even a little frenetic. Several likenesses are started, including Lady Oxford (foreground) and the journalists Hannen Swaffer (in hat) and Castlerosse (seated).

77 (following page) 'The Rake gives a cocktail party', *The Modern Rake's Progress*, London, Hutchinson, 1934

Low's notes for Rebecca West, who was writing the text: 'It is obvious that Our Hero has now become rather a swell. An expert from Heals' has fixed him up with the right carpet, a Picasso and an Epstein. . .

  'In background, lady pinching his ear, Jimmy de Rothschild. Two ladies sitting down, the green one a young version of Lady Lavery. Three young men drinking, Bob Boothby, Randolph Churchill and another. Tom Webster supporting J. H. Thomas refusing cherry from nondescript flapper. Behind, Douglas Fairbanks amusing the ladies. Over his left shoulder, Sir Denison Ross. The Rake, on his left Sir P. Sassoon, on his right three anybodies, one of whom might be Beatrice Lillie. The couple dancing are Sir Harry Preston and (only slightly) Constance Collier. At the piano, Noel Coward, over his shoulder Gertrude Lawrence. Past her, just arriving, Lady Diana Cooper and husband [Duff Cooper]. Leaning on the piano, left side, Sir Landon Ronald; right, Humbert Wolfe, a Sitwell. In foreground, Miss Jeanne Stourton sitting on floor with cigarette-holder. In right-hand corner, Cecil Beaton.

  'They are not all likenesses . . . Some are not even recognisable . . .'

78 'The Rake invests in the movies', *The Modern Rake's Progress*, London, Hutchinson, 1934

Low's notes for Rebecca West: 'Left to right: a knot of camera-men hanging about waiting. Next along, a group of producers who might be Basil Dean, Alfred Hitchcock and Anthony Asquith. The next group includes stars and "business executives" making a fuss over the Rake . . . Mae West and Greta Garbo hang on his neck . . . Charles Laughton and Jack Hulbert are in the group . . . A little apart stands the foreign Super-producer-genius, more-or-less like Korda. He wonders how the devil he will ever get anything done with such a crowd. In the right-hand corner the inevitable musicians purvey inspiration.'

79 'The Rake backs a possible world champion', *The Modern Rake's Progress*, London, Hutchinson, 1934

Low's notes for Rebecca West: 'The Rake has become a "sportsman" and has been financing another of those horizontal heavyweights of which Olde England is so prolific. Here he is matched with Carnera . . . In the front row might be some of the members of the Boxing Board of Control, Col. Myddleton, Sir W. Bass, Lord Tweedmouth, Tom Webster, Curtis Bennett, Harry Preston (it is one of his famous fight parties at which everyone smokes guinea cigars and sports uniform buttonholes. The Rake is his protégé). Poor old Lonsdale, and at the right end of the row a bookmaker suggestive of the boss of Ladbroke's ("the well-known bookmakers") seems to be making a bet. Behind, a Mosley sits between a Fannie Ward and a Lucy Houston. (Why, heaven knows – just a whim.)'

American publisher. Low called the failure of the project one of his lasting regrets.[50]

Unique among Low's books was *The Modern Rake's Progress* (1934). As the name shows, it was a Hogarthian tale of a young clerk who inherits and squanders a fortune, ending in the dole queue. Along the way he 'gives a cocktail party', 'invests in the movies', 'plunges on the turf', and makes and breaks a fashionable marriage. Low drew a double-page spread for each of the twelve episodes, packed with recognisable figures from politics, sport, the arts and letters and the London society of the 1930s. The text, sharp, malicious, brittle, was supplied in a repeat performance by 'Lynx' – Rebecca West, writing this time under her own name. Low sent a rough of each drawing for her to chew on, and with them he enclosed a fascinating key to the characters' identities (although many of them were composites). The work was serialised first in *Nash's*, which bought it before Low had sold the book rights.

What Low originally had in mind, as long ago as 1925, was rather different from the Rake. Beaverbrook, writing to acknowledge his complimentary copy, remarked opaquely: 'I am glad that the Rake does not look like anyone I know.'[51] Low's initial plan, as Beaverbrook doubtless knew, was to hang his 'pageant of London life' upon the Prince of Wales. The idea struck when he found himself playing a round of golf right behind the Prince on holiday in Biarritz. When he started to plan in detail, the problems naturally ramified. But just a touch of the Prince perhaps remains in one or two of the compositions.

Low took tremendous pains with the drawings, most of which are highly complex. Moreover they were done in colour and would be unique for that if for no other reason. Apart from a few book jackets, magazine covers and individual items Low was exclusively a black-and-white artist. The project ate into his leisure and holiday time, but he enjoyed every minute of it.[52] So, plainly, did Rebecca West. The book was handsomely produced and not expensive. Low took three-quarters of the royalties and West one-quarter. The reviews, from Brisbane to Calcutta, seem almost uniformly generous in retrospect, but for some reason Rebecca West was incensed and it is plain from much later correspondence that the book's sales were disappointing.[53] As to the pictures, William Rothenstein told Low they should be in the Tate.[54] The improbably named Lessing J. Rosenwald of Jenkinstown, Pennsylvania, put out feelers about buying them in 1941, possibly after seeing some in a touring exhibition. Low's friendly reply said that besides feeling they represented some of his best work, 'the War has given the series something of the value of a historical document, and my own wish is that one day it may find an appropriate home in some museum in London itself.'[55] The pictures have been exhibited quite often but remain in private hands.

Low's interest in the cinema went beyond the mere absorption of the moving image as a means of relaxation. He and his wife were discerning cinema-goers. His feeling for the unexplored potential of the medium even led him to make the apparently extravagant claim that Walt Disney was the most significant figure in graphic art since Leonardo. In *Fantasia*, he argued, Disney 'lifts the art of drawing movement right out of the "comic" and essays for the first time serious studies on the higher plane.' All the 'emotional elements' combined in a conventional 'static' painting could now be explored in movement. This was the sort of opportunity that the inventive mind of Leonardo, if alive today, would have seized on. 'He would be in his back room inventing simplifications of animating processes and projection devices.'[56]

Low himself flirted with the possibilities of animation at least twice. Encouraged by Beaverbrook when he was still at the *Star*, he discussed the possibility of providing drawings for Pathé which could be animated and attached to the weekly newsreels. When it became clear that Low would have to do his own animation ('There are only about three men in America who can do the job . . . and none here,' Beaverbrook asserted, rightly or wrongly), the project foundered.[57] Ten years later Gasparcolor, a film company whose production manager was Humphrey Jennings, put up a similar idea. Low made three drawings 'in plain flat colour' for a cartoon about new types of air-raid precaution. There were houses with rubber roofs, off which bombs would bounce; fly-papers to catch aeroplanes; and 'a mad-looking professor wearing a peculiar-looking straw hat'. This time a trial film does seem to have been made, but it did not lead to others.[58]

From time to time people suggested animating Colonel Blimp. This never happened, but the name and appearance of the character were taken up in a wartime film by Michael Powell and Emeric Pressburger, *The Life and Death of Colonel Blimp* (1943). At the time this was the longest and most expensive film ever made in a British studio. Low of course had to be approached for his agreement. He gave it on condition that the film character was shown to be stupid in the end, stupidity being the essence

78

JOAN,

THE FLAPPER.

"JOAN"
Stock Mannerism
Powdering her nose

80 & **81**   Sketches of 'Joan', unpublished, *c.* 1928

These pages from Low's sketchbooks show him striving to capture movement on paper. How to get Joan's hips to 'wiggle'? How to translate dog into powder puff? Low admired Disney's inventiveness: '. . . a growing understanding of the meaning of observed movement and therefore greatly increased powers of creating imagined movement' ('Leonardo da Disney' in *New Republic*, 5 January 1942).

"JOAN"
HER WALK.

of Blimp, and that the producers took all the responsibility. The latter proved to be no joke. Official suspicion prevented the release of Laurence Olivier from the services to play the leading role, which Roger Livesey took instead. Then, although the film sentimentalised Blimp as a well-meaning, determined type with a VC from the Boer War, there was enough mockery of his resistance to change for Churchill, who attended the first night, to oppose its export. It would be 'disastrously bad propaganda', said the *Daily Mail*. In the end it went abroad in an altered version, with Blimp depicted on the American posters as a twinkling old womaniser. Low enjoyed watching the film being made, and he had long ago become inured to misunderstandings and controversy attaching to the Blimp symbol.[59]

Low became increasingly well-known from the late 1920s onwards. This was partly due to a simple readiness for publicity (the Low self-confidence again?). Some months after he joined the *Evening Standard*, for example, the paper published a full-page article on his boyhood by his mother.[60] No doubt it was ghosted, and approved by Low, and it was one of a series called 'Makers of Men'. None the less it needs a certain disposition, at age thirty-seven, to welcome an article by one's mum, complete with photographs of oneself dressed as 'Boy Blue' at age three and with confidences about how she hoped one might become a clergyman. He willingly accepted invitations to give talks and after-dinner speeches. He cooperated in such ventures as the *Star*'s election-night service in 1923, when his on-the-spot cartoons were to be flashed onto the large screen at Selfridges store in Oxford Street on which the results were announced. (Bad weather in fact prevented it.) When he visited his Scottish roots, the story was written up in the Dundee papers as well as in the *Star* and *Daily News*.

These occasional items reinforced the more regular familiarity of Low's appearances in his own cartoons. The internal commentator is a cartooning commonplace. Low's contemporary on the *Daily Express*, Strube, had a famous 'little man'. But Strube was no self-publicist. His little man was an abstraction, an Everyman: Low's was a recognisable version of himself. Captions, or more often comments within the frame, might address the reader directly. When Low appeared in company, with Joan Bull or Blimp for instance, the address would be indirect. Readers either shared with Low the receipt of the Colonel's aphorisms or shared those of Low with Joan. In each case, the cartoonist engaged himself personally with his audience, not simply confiding in them

GOOD MORNING! DO I WANT A MODEL?

NOW THAT FLAPPERS ARE SO IMPORTANT, I SUPPOSE ONE SHOULD DO A LITTLE STUDY FROM THE LIFE.

SO YOU'RE TO HAVE THE VOTE, HEY? TUT TUT!

Joan Bull

YOU YOUNG PEOPLE — LACKING THE RIPE WISDOM OF EXPERIENCE. BOYS OF 21 TOO! DEAR, DEAR!

The Hand that Rocks the Cradle Rules the World

NOT THAT OLDER PEOPLE SHOULD HAVE VOTES, THOUGH. WHAT KNOW THEY OF THE NEEDS OF A YOUNG PEOPLE'S WORLD?

NO PEOPLE OF ANY AGE SHOULD HAVE VOTES IF THEY DON'T KNOW WHAT THEY'RE UP TO, AND, IF THEY DO, THEY SHOULDN'T HAVE VOTES BECAUSE THEY ARE OUT OF TOUCH WITH THE PEOPLE WHO DON'T.

The White Misses' Burden

RESPONSIBILITIES

TAXES FROM MR CHURCHILL, DRAT HIM.

WHAT THIS COUNTRY NEEDS IS A BENEVOLENT DESPOTISM, DEAREST,

WITH ME AS THE BENEVOLENT DESPOT.

LOW HAS A NEW MODEL.

but inviting them – challenging them, virtually – to respond. 'Personally I am an arguer,' Low said in a radio discussion in 1940. 'I talk to my work. Once or twice at my studio I have had people knock at my door to ask whom I am having a row with, and it has been just me bawling at someone as I drew him in a cartoon.' Low wanted the readers to be part of his argument. But unhappily, he wrote, 'few people take a cartoon as a link in a consecutive argument – today's instalment, to be continued tomorrow'.[61]

The urge to provoke, engage, set an argument going, is extremely strong in Low's cartoons. Where he himself appears as protagonist, reaction was bound to be to himself in person too. Features such as 'Low and I' and the 'diary' elements of the Topical Budget put the focus even more directly, of course, on the cartoonist's person.

From time to time Low did indeed get a 'dialogue' going. The reaction to one cartoon – about Marie Stopes and birth control, for example; or years later the emotional excesses of Queen Elizabeth's coronation – might provide material for a second or third, in which the cartoonist would as like as not be the butt.

82 'Low has a new model', *Evening Standard*, 23 January 1928

Joan Bull became a regular member of Low's cast of characters. She never lost that look of bemusement at finding herself with a vote in a hostile and largely masculine world.

'I have not given Joan Bull a sense of humour, and if anybody is expecting her to produce cleverly witty sayings they will, I am afraid, be disappointed, because I have created her upon what I consider to be the mass type of woman. Her remarks are undiluted by sophistication, but she usually goes straight to the point. The trees do not hide her view of the wood.' (Low, *Manchester Evening News*, 14 February 1928)

81

TAKING THE SALUTE.

(Despite the much discussed "cuts" the War Services Estimates still total a stupendous sum to be paid by the taxpayer.)

83 'Taking the salute', *Evening Standard*, early 1930s

When the threat of the Fascist dictators became extreme, Low was to call for greater and quicker rearmament. In this early cartoon, however, arms expenditure seems an extravagance. Even his dog Musso cannot bear to watch the marchpast of the service chiefs with their inordinate appetite for Low's taxes.

The public reaction to a cartoon might often make news and provoke editorial comment in distant continents. In the letters columns Low appeared all the time. The *Evening Standard* made a regular feature out of readers' reactions to him, and Low used to join in the correspondence ('Suddenly the body rose and joined in the inquest,' began one of his contributions).

All such reactions were probably increased by Low's vaunted independence from editorial policy. The 'harmony' between Beaverbrook and Low must have accentuated the cartoons' personal element too. What made Low's work much more impressive than his contemporaries', commented the novelist Howard Spring in 1936 (admittedly in the *Evening Standard*) was 'the sense that grows on the beholder, seeing it week by week, of the personality of the artist'.[62]

Obviously Low could not predict all the quarters from which reactions might come. Could he help it if the Billiwog became

OLD LOW'S ALMANACK.   *PROPHECIES FOR 1931*

84   '*Old Low's Almanack*. Prophecies for 1931: Attempted Revolution in Dublin', *Evening Standard*, 6 December 1930

A cartoon about Irish Catholic attitudes to the works of Marie Stopes on birth control was bound to make readers reach for their pens. Marie Stopes herself wrote to David Low (9 December): 'Your drawings, & the penetration they portray, have often delighted & amused me; but as you can imagine I was never more delighted or amused than by your caricature in the Evening Standard of the Revolution in Dublin . . . I am afraid you will get into terribly hot water about it . . .'

Among the letters published in the *Evening Standard* were the following:

Sir, – 'Old Low's Almanack' in Saturday's 'Evening Standard' is perfect! It is a bright light in this (mentally and morally) foggy world. More power to Old Low's elbow and genius. I am sending a bunch of those cartoons with Christmas cards to America. . . .

Sir, – I have received a number of letters this morning from members asking me to protest in the name of the National University Club against the bad taste of the cartoon in your issue of Saturday last. I shall bring the matter before my committee at a meeting to-night. . . .

Sir, – What a pity Low doesn't give us a few more Irish masterpieces from time to time. The English,

Scots and Welsh come in for most of his hard knocks – and enjoy them. We mere Irish would welcome an odd lambasting, if it were so happy and riotous as the last . . .

Sir, – It was with great regret that I as a reader of your paper saw the cartoon in the 'Evening Standard'. It may well be described as a 'Low' cartoon.

Sir, – May an Irish reader of the 'Evening Standard' thank Low for the best laugh in 12 months? Dubliners are more comely than depicted and affect a more vivid and witty idiom than the quaint and archaic one reported . . .

IN DIFFERENT WORLDS.

85 'In different worlds', *Evening Standard*, 17 April 1934

Low depicts Neville Chamberlain, supercilious and haughty, holding forth about 'the nation's money box' while the workforce starves beside the idle engines of production. The Chancellor of the Exchequer and his colleagues inhabit a dream world detached from reality. This kind of contemptuous comment must have been quite out of sympathy with the attitudes of most *Evening Standard* readers.

news, or if he became entangled in a row about conscription? Was he to blame, if farmworkers handed their MP a bunch of thistles symbolising the Government's farm policy and told him to give it to Lloyd George for the Coalition Ass? If an attaché at the Italian Embassy protested to the *Standard* about Low's dog having the name 'Musso', was it Low's fault?

Low's publicity grew strongly through the 1930s. It became fame: his work was in the Tate Gallery. It became celebrity: his image was in Madame Tussaud's. (In the days before TV, the significance of the waxworks was greater than now.) Reviewers regularly called him a national asset, an institution. He was the talk of the town, said J. B. Priestley. A letter addressed to plain 'Low' reached him safely. In discreet advertisements, he endorsed Du Maurier cigarettes, alongside Maurice Chevalier and Sir Henry Lytton. 'My mail was absurdly large. We were surfeited with invitations.'[63] Christmas gifts came from strangers. He appeared in newspaper diary columns. In 1930 he was the

MR PRESIDENT

defendant in a widely reported mock trial at the London School
of Economics to raise money for charity. His prosecutor was A. P.
Herbert, who wrote it up in *Punch*.[64]

When Low visited the United States in 1936, for the first time
since 1919, he was news. His own news sense led him to say that
he was on the lookout for six great personalities but could not
reveal them except in such terms as 'prizefighter' or 'politician'
because it would put them on their guard.[65] When the drawings
were done and the identities disclosed, of course, there was more
publicity. One of them proved to be the President, Franklin
Roosevelt, with whom Low had a private audience. Low was
celebrated enough in New York in 1938 to be included in a long
piece of doggerel listing people to whom the *New Yorker* wished
Christmas greetings.

There were also commercial spinoffs from Low's cartoons.
Blimp featured on bath tiles. A tear-off 'Musso' calendar for 1939
was produced by Raphael Tuck, using the weather-report drawings done for the *Star* years earlier. Stuffed Musso dogs were
manufactured, and a stuffed Pindar the Panda. (Pindar illustrated
a children's feature by Peter Howard in the *Evening Standard* in
1939.) A stuffed Blimp would doubtless have sold. The confec-
tioners Batgers wanted to make sweets in the shape of Muzzler
the dictator, for sale at the seaside in 1938. (Whatever would psy-
chologists make of that?) 'Low is so much public property that

87 'Dog days', calendar, 1939

Raphael Tuck produced this tear-off calendar for which Low resurrected 'Musso' drawings from as far back as his days on the *Star*.

88 Menu design for Parliamentary Press Gallery Dinner, 1935

'He loved it. He had been playing that gag about simple farmer Baldwin with his pipe and pigs so long that he almost came to believe it himself.' (*Autobiography*, p. 258)

MR GANDHI in confinement spends his time spinning and making cloth.

A SHROUD FOR LIBERTY

it is difficult to say anything fresh about him,' said *The Times*, discussing an exhibition of his work in London in 1937.[66]

It is not easy to be precise about celebrity. But its products are not all public. For instance, Low became a member of several exclusive dining clubs in the late 1920s. There were the Omar Khayyam (to the memory of Fitzgerald), the Titmarsh (for Thackeray fans) and the Odd Volumes. His clubs in the larger sense were the National Liberal and the Savile. (He was put up for the latter by the cartoonist Bert Thomas.) Members of 'the Sette of Odd Volumes', which met at the Savoy, each took a title. Letters to Low began 'Dear Exaggerator'. He was much in demand as a designer of menus.

How much did he really see of the other celebrities with whom he mixed? The terms of friendship are presumably different for the celebrated from the rest of us. It is difficult to catch the exact flavour of Low's life, especially the interaction of the professional and the private. How far, for example, were people chary of him?

89 'A shroud for liberty', *Evening Standard*, 11 August 1942

Gandhi was imprisoned in 1942 for endorsing the Indian Congress Party's campaign to force the British to 'Quit India'. Congress was declared an illegal organisation.

When Low met Gandhi in 1931 for a portrait-caricature sitting he had found him 'squatting on floor near fire, spinning wheel on right, little brown head with short grey hair peeping elfishly out of copious homespun blanket – large hands and feet – skin warm and pleasant to touch'. Eleven years later he is able to draw on those visual memories to produce an arresting likeness.

"... ABOVE ALL, MY DEAR LAVAL, WE MUST CONTINUE TO STAND FIRM...".

"DISCUSSIONS ARE PROCEEDING"

90 'Discussions are proceeding', *Evening Standard*, 29 August 1935

Across the years Low drew Mussolini as lunatic, rabid dog, fool, coward, puppet and *poseur*. There was no middle ground and little let-up. In this cartoon Baldwin, Laval and the League are criticised for their weakness in not stopping Mussolini from invading Abyssinia. The strength of the composition lies in the tautness and momentum of the headlong rush.

Low used to tell the story of a 'tribal chieftain' (the details fluctuated) before whom a stranger who could draw likenesses was one day brought. 'Draw me,' said the chieftain; and he drew him so well that the man was buried the next day. Capturing a likeness is a sort of magic. The politician seeing Low across a room knew that Low might be 'noting' him; might put him in a cartoon; might ridicule or, in his own mind, misrepresent him. Writing journalists have an ambiguous status as observer/participants too. But many of them are reporters not commentators, and they lack the crucial graphic dimension, the personification intrinsic to caricature. When Low visited Max Beerbohm he saw a man of fine pointed extremities and sharp perception. 'I recognised immediately the occupational characteristic of the caricaturist. The slight detachment produced by trying to do two things at once – concentrate on the particular while expanding on the general.' Low, the observer, felt himself observed, and was perhaps a little chary too.[67]

"CORRECT ATTITUDES" IN SPAIN.

Whatever may have been people's feelings about the peculiar power of the caricaturist, Low's geniality and clubbability ensured him a wide social circle. He had increasingly too to discriminate among the public political commitments urged upon him.

Low's standard reason for not joining political groups was that he could be most effective by remaining an independent critic. For the same reason he generally refused the frequent requests in the 1930s to illustrate pamphlets or let cartoons be reproduced. Most of these came from leftist and anti-Fascist groups. So Canon Dick Sheppard, a noted churchman, had to do without a Low cartoon for his peace propaganda in 1936. So did the London Federation of Peace Councils, the No More War Movement, the Hampstead Peace Council and the Hampstead Spanish Relief Committee. But distinctions could be drawn. In May 1933 Low became a director of the *New Statesman*, an explicitly leftist magazine 'independent' only in the sense that it was not under party control. Low thus wore a definite leftist label, and he added

91 '"Correct attitudes" in Spain', *Evening Standard*, 5 August 1936

Low was a strong supporter of the Republican cause in the Spanish Civil War. He repeatedly drew Franco as a fledgling Fascist dictator, particularly when allied with Mussolini. Here Low criticises the mealy-mouthed official policy expressed by the Foreign Secretary Eden and by Blum, the French Premier.

89

his name to the long and distinguished lists of signatories to letters to *The Times*, chiefly about the worsening international situation. Sometimes these were reprinted as news items, abroad as well as at home.[68]

He joined a few organisations: Friends of the Spanish Republic; the International Association of Writers for the Defence of Culture. About Spain he made a rare speech at a public meeting protesting against the Government's non-intervention policy. He joined the committee seeking the release of defendants acquitted after the Reichstag fire in 1933. Shortly after the Council for Civil Liberties (later the National Council) was founded in the same year he agreed to become a vice-president (one of more than fifty). In November he repeated for the CCL his mock trial experience, this time to highlight opposition to the Government's Sedition Bill. Low was defendant and Kingsley Martin was a soldier allegedly seduced from his duty by a Low cartoon ridiculing the army. The actor Miles Malleson was a policeman, and the editor of the *News Chronicle*, Aylmer Vallance, was the judge.

One source which conveys something of the activity of the cartoonist as famous man is a note Low made of his professional expenses for January to March 1936. The details for March are these:

March		£.	s.	d.
3	Lunch to a publisher [Cresset Press] re contract for new book		18.	6
4	Lunch to an ambassador and his wife [Maisky] (information) 6 persons	5.	8.	0
5	All-England Badminton Championships		10.	0
10	Lunch to a Cabinet Minister, an eminent economist and two artists (information)	3.	15.	0
12	'Rhodes of Africa' film (for reference)		7.	0
17	Lunch to famous writer [Alec Waugh] (re a collaboration)	1.	1.	6
	Taxis to and from St James's Palace for Conference [of League of Nations]		7.	9
22	[Sir Oswald] Mosley meeting at Albert Hall		10.	0
23	Lunch to an international journalist and a foreign statesman (re League Conference)	1.	9.	6

IT WORKED AT THE REICHSTAG — WHY NOT HERE?

Supper to theatrical magnate
[Leon M. Lion], an ambassador
[Maisky] and economist [Keynes] (for
information)   2. 12. 0

26   Omar Khayyam [Dining Club]
      Dinner (for portraits)   15. 0

27   Return fare to Aintree (Grand
      National)   3. 11. 0

30   Dinner to two Labour politicians
      [J. F. Horrobin was one] (information
      re party movements)   2. 11. 1

92 'It worked at the Reichstag –
why not here?', *Evening Standard*,
18 November 1933

Low's real target is not Hitler but the
cowardice of League members who
funked their collective duty to
discipline him. Glimpsed at the
windows are Mussolini (at this stage
held to have some restraining
influence over Hitler), Simon and
Daladier. The weapon of economic
sanctions is available but unused. The
swastika, later to become a knee-jerk
hate symbol, is drawn back to front.

A quite different measure of fame was the reaction of the Axis
powers to Low's ridicule. Soon after Hitler came to power, Low
drew a cartoon of a bonfire outside the League of Nations building, with Hitler saying 'It worked at the Reichstag – why not
here?' Beaverbrook's newspapers were immediately banned from
Germany. The cartoon, of course, was then printed around the

THE GIRLS HE LEFT BEHIND HIM.

93 'The girls he left behind him', *Evening Standard*, 10 May 1935

Goebbels, Hitler and Goering are only too happy to see Mussolini's ambitions directed away from central Europe into the deserts of Abyssinia. The cartoon provoked an immediate ban on the *Evening Standard* and *Manchester Guardian* in Italy.

world. Earlier in the year the *Evening Standard* and *Manchester Guardian* were banned in Italy too because of a cartoon about Hitler's attitude to Mussolini's expansionist policy in Abyssinia (The girls he left behind him – 11 May). After Beaverbrook visited Berlin in 1935 the bans on the *Daily* and *Sunday Express* were lifted, but not on the *Standard*. Feeling continued high enough – in Beaverbrook's view, at any rate – for him to advise Low in 1936 not to go into Germany while holidaying in Austria, unless 'at the express invitation of the German Government'.[69]

Other papers were banned as well – the *Daily Herald* and the *New Statesman*, for instance. The British press was a constant source of complaint in Berlin. The question of Low was taken up with the Foreign Secretary, Lord Halifax, when Halifax visited Berchtesgaden privately in 1937 for talks with the German leaders. Hitler was said to be personally incensed by Low's attacks. On his return, Halifax put the position to Low over lunch with Beaverbrook's aide, Michael Wardell. While sceptical whether his cartoons made the smallest difference to German policy, Low 'played it in a less personal key' for a few weeks. Nazi troops

swiftly annexed Austria. Low felt his restraint had been point-less.[70] The German Government shortly made a formal protest about him to the Foreign Office – another source of worldwide publicity, which incidentally went to help build up Low's regular syndication in non-totalitarian Europe.

A different measure again of fame was the natural history of Colonel Blimp. Blimp took on a life of his own long before he was put on the cinema screen. He was introduced on 21 April 1934, in the first Topical Budget. Eighteen months later *The Times* noted that he had already 'passed into the mythology of our country, to share the timeless existence of beings like Sherlock Holmes'. When Low broadcast his 'auto-obituary' in a radio series in 1936, the *Listener* version was headed 'Bereavement of Colonel Blimp', not 'Demise of Low'. He was included in the Universal English Dictionary in the same year. By the end of 1938 he was being translated into twenty-four languages. C. S. Lewis, among others, said that Blimp had been *discovered*, not *invented*; a view cheerfully shared by Low, who wrote a syndicated article ('Does Blimp Exist?') describing how they first 'met' in a Turkish bath.[71]

94 'Col. Blimp speaks out' and 'Col. Blimp's lead', *Evening Standard, c.* 1934

Hans Christian Andersen gave us the Emperor whose nakedness was exposed by childish innocence. Low's steambath Blimp was a reworking of the same idea – with Low, of course, as the perceptive child.

The appeal of Blimp was that he meant something to everyone: but not the *same* thing. Harold Nicolson doubted in 1942 whether he could find seven or eight people who really held Blimp's views; while the American journalist Ray Daniell, at the same time and in the same city, reported that 'It's impossible to live in London long without encountering the Old Colonel.'[72] Blimp's potency as a symbol is explored further in the next chapter. But it was the universality of his appeal, coupled with the individuality of his meaning, that made him so quickly more famous than his creator. 'They speak of Shylock,' a journalist sagely remarked, 'who know little of Shakespeare.'[73]

Certainly Low took pains to protect his copyright and his own definition of the character. He repeatedly wrote letters and articles emphasising Blimp's stupidity: 'He does NOT represent a coherent reactionary outlook so much as slapdash stupidity.' Yet some commentators, affected by Blimp's apparent warmhearted sincerity, persisted in interpreting him otherwise. Low refused to let people put him on the stage, except in a Farjeon revue which he endorsed retroactively; nor to exploit his potential in other forms, whether it was the repertoire of a concert party entertainer or the peg for a series of articles entitled 'Says Colonel Blimp'.

The outbreak of the Second World War changed Low's routine, especially once the Blitz started. He began working at home. He could not get brushes and improvised with his own hair. He got his cartoon ready earlier in the day or even, if he could, several days ahead. Knowing he was on the Gestapo blacklist, he made arrangements for the safety of his family if there was an invasion, and he shaved off the beard which by now made him recognisable in the street. All this is amusingly described in the autobiography.

The cartoonist's task in wartime is in some ways simplified. His energies can focus on one grand theme and provide his audience with emotional release. Cartoons like 'All behind you, Winston' and 'Very well, alone' 'practically drew themselves at white heat'.[74] As someone who had been proved resoundingly correct about Hitler, moreover, Low found himself with a reputation not simply as a cartoonist but, on the international scene at least, a prophet. Such fame could get in the way. When his drawings of Nazi leaders on trial at Nuremberg appeared in the *Manchester Guardian* after the war, several readers complained. They were too reminiscent for comfort 'of the days when the conquerors paraded their captives through the streets for the mob to spit and jeer at'. Low had no such ulterior motive. But the

94

ALL BEHIND YOU, WINSTON

95 'All behind you, Winston', *Evening Standard*, 14 May 1940

Churchill replaced Chamberlain on 10 May 1940. Dunkirk lay ahead. Low's 'flying wedge' of politicians fall resolutely in behind Churchill. Low is careful to stress that this is a 'national unity' government by placing three important Labour figures next to him. Attlee, Bevin and Morrison, indeed, form the centrepiece. Behind them come Chamberlain, Greenwood, Halifax, Sinclair, Duff Cooper, Alexander, Amery and Eden. Strictly speaking, as Angus Calder suggests, 'to depict reality [Low] should have shown Churchill walking apart and ahead with a small group of confidants, Ernest Bevin striding away by himself not far behind them, and the rest following in double file' (*The People's War*, London, Panther, 1971, p. 115).

Low often used this arrowhead formation to portray a sense of unstoppable power.

VERY WELL, ALONE

96 'Very well, alone', *Evening Standard*, 18 June 1940

Low pictures Britain defiant and alone after the fall of Dunkirk. He whips up the sea to mirror the waves of enemy bombs. 'I tingled when I drew it,' he recalled in 1961; and in his *Autobiography* he wrote: 'The anguish which infused the great occasions imposed a pregnant simplicity on their interpretation' (p. 333).

trouble was, the paper rejoined, that he was so famous that when he drew a straight sketch 'it becomes in the popular mind a caricature'.[75]

Low might be thought an obvious candidate for official propaganda work. 'The cartoon he did the other day was worth a ton of this printed stuff,' said an MP in a debate on the Ministry of Information in 1939.[76] Low's peacetime objection to 'commitment' surely would not apply now. Yet things did not quite work out, due largely, one suspects, to his independent cast of mind and piano-case practices. He spent time on two Ministry ventures which came to nothing through administrative bungling, and he

LOW'S NUEREMBERG SKETCHBOOK — № 1

97 'Low's Nueremberg
Sketchbook (No. 1)', *Evening
Standard*, 12 December 1945

'Sketchbook in hand, I am examining
Goering meticulously when he turns
his gaze and hooks my eye. After
about twenty seconds of mutual
glaring it dawns upon me that he is
trying to stare me down. The
childish vanity of it! How silly! (I
win, by the way.)' (*Autobiography*,
p. 360)

EUROPE'S VALENTINE.

98 'Europe's Valentine', *Star*,
13 February 1926

Mussolini, in a speech to the Italian
Chamber of Deputies on 6 February
1926, had violently attacked what he
called 'German interference' in the
Italian-controlled Tyrol and the
upper Trentino. In a flamboyant
tirade he had promised immediate
reprisals should Italian 'dignity,
strength and moral-force' be
threatened by German pressure.

   Low early recognised Mussolini as
a demagogue and never changed his
line of attack.

In the image:

NOTICE
THE REVOLUTION IS OVER
THE CONSTRUCTIVE SOCIALISM PART OF THE NATIONAL-SOCIALIST PROGRAMME IS POSTPONED INDEFINITELY. ANYONE REMINDING THE LEADER OF IT WILL BE TREATED AS A COMMUNIST.
HEIL HITLER!
DOUBLE CROOKED CROSS № 275

IN THE LAND OF THE NASTIES.

99 'In the land of the Nasties', *Evening Standard*, 27 July 1933

Figures to be mocked more than feared, Hitler and Goering are shown as prisoners – Goering cramped by drug addiction, and Hitler tied to the business interests supporting the National Socialist Party. At this time it was easy to regard the top Nazis as puppets, manipulated by forces more powerful than them in Germany. 'Nasty' must still have seemed a fresh enough pun to be worth making.

felt that the potential of cartoon propaganda was not being taken seriously enough. He contributed to a leaflet to be dropped over Germany, to a few posters and to other 'trivialities'. His advice was sought, too, on the best way of depicting the Nazis. 'Ridicule,' he replied. 'I have been looking at some "anti-Nazi" cartoons from Denmark current in 1937 showing Nazi leaders as dreadful powerful brutes. That kind of thing no doubt had the effect of building up the idea that Hitler was too, too, too powerful to resist . . . Personally, I know that the cartoons of mine that got under their skins most were those which made them look like damned fools.'[77]

Chiefly, then, Low left his cartoons to make their own propaganda. He published some extremely successful Penguin paperback anthologies. The first, *Europe since Versailles* (1940), sold a quick quarter of a million copies. Characteristically, Low decided to do it as a piece of popular education – the kind of book the curious young Low of forty years ago might have studied in order

STEPPING STONES TO GLORY.

to make sense of the slide from one world war to another. *Europe at War* (1941) and *The World at War* (1941) followed in the same format. An American anthology, *Low on the War*, appeared in 1941 too, and Cresset Press, publisher of the prewar large-format anthologies, brought out *Low's War Cartoons* (1941) in hard covers.

From 1941 to 1944 Low also broadcast topical monthly talks, that were bound to be propagandist in a morale-boosting way, on the BBC Pacific Service. Many were reprinted in the *Listener*. He built up a connection too with the Sunday edition of the *New York Times*, joining the band of writers interpreting the British and Americans to each other as their cooperation grew. Low's antipodean background gave him an effective element of detachment both in these broadcasts and the articles. He wrote crisp prose, fresh with the wit and imagery to be expected from such an inventive cartoonist. Beaverbrook used to tease him that his decision to be a cartoonist was a great loss to journalism.

100 'Stepping stones to glory', *Evening Standard*, 8 July 1936

Three years later Low sensed that Hitler's momentum would become unstoppable unless governments adopt firmer measures. Low uses one of his strongly diagonal designs to accentuate Hitler's rise.

101 'Would you oblige me with a match, please?', *Evening Standard*, 25 February 1938

Muzzler, Low's composite dictator, is setting up an ineffectual Chamberlain for destruction. Eden, whose picture Chamberlain holds, had just resigned from the Cabinet in protest over the continuing policy of appeasement.

WOULD YOU OBLIGE ME WITH A MATCH PLEASE ?

THE RED CARPET.

RENDEZVOUS

103   'Rendezvous', *Evening Standard*, 20 September 1939

The Nazi–Soviet Pact was signed on 24 August 1939. 'Britain and France were dragged to war under such uninspiring and disadvantageous circumstances that it seemed hardly possible for them to win. What a situation! In gloomy wrath at missed opportunity and human stupidity I drew the bitterest cartoon of my life, RENDEZVOUS, the meeting of the "Enemy of the People" [sic] with the "Scum of the Earth" in the smoking ruins of Poland' (*Autobiography*, p. 320). Of all Low's cartoons, this has been reproduced most often.

102   (opposite) 'The red carpet', *Evening Standard*, 14 June 1935

Low was not fooled by the puppet governments established by the conquering Japanese forces in northern China. He knew enough of European dictatorships to be aware that Japan's military regime was a comparable threat to international order.

THE ANGELS OF PEACE DESCEND ON BELGIUM

104 'The angels of peace descend on Belgium', *Evening Standard*, 10 June 1940

In the wake of dictatorship comes terror. Low depicts Nazi Gestapo leader Himmler with his henchmen as black 'angels'. The peace they bring will be the quiet of the grave for potential leaders of the Resistance.

A more unusual and shortlived broadcasting experiment was Low's 'radio cartoons'. He described them later as a monumental flop.[78] This was presumably true. Read now, the scripts look rather as though they were ahead of their time. There is a sound of the *Goon Show* in them. The signature tune, to judge by the *Radio Times* description, anticipated Gerard Hoffnung. 'Not a play, not a cross-talk act,' Low later explained. 'We tried to get in through the ear the same effect you got through the eye from a newspaper cartoon. The chief difficulty experienced was of tempo. The public are accustomed to hearing quick-fire gagging, i.e. a series of gags tumbling out one after the other, innocuous

THE FAIRIES BRING THEIR GIFTS

and disconnected; and the listener can come in on this at any time and pick it up quickly . . . He knows how to listen, in other words. But the development of a satirical theme, with gags containing cartoon meaning, cannot be listened to so quickly. The listener is not used to it. It requires more attention.'[79] The 'cartoons' lasted three minutes and were tacked on to a weekly news magazine on the Home Service. They were billed as 'experimental' in the advance publicity, so honour was saved when they were abandoned.

Here is Low's script for one of them:

105 'The fairies bring their gifts', *Evening Standard*, 30 December 1943

A gruesome echo of the 'angels of peace . . .' came three years later. Now the three black angels are visiting Nazi Germany. Hitler hides under the cot (signifying the new year 1944). The baby, rather grimly, reminds us that Germany will eventually be reduced to sending children to war.

Optimism On The Eastern Front
Cartoon by Low

(The keynote of the whole scene is COLD. Sound background should be a miserable moaning wind. Göbbels' voice should have an acid cheerfulness, in contrast to the deadly gloom of the German soldier. His stress on the word cold *should be longer drawn out with every repetition until it merges in the howl of the wind.)*

ANNOUNCER: Göbbels deplores pessimism on Eastern Front. Demands that Nazi soldiers look on bright side. Göbbels to make personal 'cheer-up' Tour.

GÖBBELS [*brightly*]: Here ve are, back at der Front.
GERMAN SOLDIER [*sourly*]: Back to Front. Dodt's right. It's coldt. Brrr.

Dollop. Thud with chunk of icicles.

GÖB: Vot's for dinner? Snow soup and frozen mud pies? Excellent! Much better than Rommel's baked dust.
G.S.: Ve iss coldt. Brrr! Our clothes and boots iss full of holes.
GÖB: Good. Aind't this a holy war?
G.S.: Ve iss coldt. 2,000 of our comrades were killed yesterday.
GÖB: Grand. More Russian territory occupied.
G.S.: It's *coldt*. Und ve were pushed back twenty-five miles yesterday.
GÖB: Splendid! Our victorious troops are returning in triumph.
G.S.: It's coldt. Und here iss der enemy!

Rattle of machine guns rapidly rising to crescendo of battle noises.
  ZIP   CRASH   BOOM

GÖB: Wow! Aind't it hot!

With the turn of the tide and talk of postwar reconstruction Low became more controversial again. In the 1945 general election he and Beaverbrook had never been farther apart politically. Low's radical sympathies were all with Labour. Beaverbrook was trumpeting for Churchill and the Tories. When Labour swept into office, Beaverbrook was blamed more than ever for tolerating Low.

'The war had changed a lot of things. The face of Humanity.

ON THE HIGHER LEVEL

The *Evening Standard.* Me.' Of its nearly 400 pages, the autobiography, published in 1956, gives less than thirty to the postwar years. That could be just impatience. 'The fact is,' Low wrote to Kingsley Martin, 'after tossing off 150,000 words, I am sick, almost physically sick, of writing.'[80] But the deeper explanation, surely, is that for the first time in his career Low and his times were out of joint. 'How many of us think that Low is at his best in the present dispensation?' asked *The Times* in 1947. The *Economist* wrote: 'Low will not be really happy again until there is a Conservative Government to poke fun at.' Joss, the cartoonist of the *Star*, wrote that Low's political line was less clear-cut and sharp: his humour was duller while 'the sermons have

106 'On the higher level', *Evening Standard*, 26 June 1945

A figure based on Rodin's 'Thinker' ponders the real issues of the 1945 general election. Low is contemptuous of Conservative attempts to clutter the campaign with trivia. He brands Beaverbrook as one of the chief offenders. Even Churchill is included as one of the 'child-minds', complete with bonnet and nappy. 'Diogenes' Low retreated into a barrel for the campaign.

"GIVING A LEAD"

107 'Giving a lead', *Evening Standard*, 12 August 1947

Like many commentators, Low was impatient with Attlee's cautious leadership. Once again he uses a 'flying wedge' to make his point.

remained'.[81] Cartoons in the early postwar years certainly *nudge* the Government. The trades unions are often criticised for lack of 'realism' or excessive wage demands. But Joss's comment seems fair.

By early 1948 Low clearly felt he wanted a change. When the editor of the *Evening Standard* told him his space would have to be cut from four columns to three ('we are having further to compress our Features and cut the news'), Low's reply summed up his mood: 'This is a dismal prospect for me, who wants to DRAW, and for my reputation, which must suffer a decline here and wherever E.S. syndications go.' He invoked the contract clause entitling him to three months' holiday abroad. He had already been travelling around Europe; now he wanted to revisit the United States. 'I have been feeling a bit stale since the war ended, . . . and now seems a good time.'[82]

So off went Low (with his wife) to cover the American presidential campaign. Their expenses were covered by *Time-Life*,

"NO CHANGE"—WITH A DIFFERENCE

who had first option on his drawings. At the Republican convention he enjoyed using his old Australian experience 'in fading myself in and out of places where I should not have been'.[83] He was fascinated by Hollywood and was fêted by the National Cartoonists' Society.

The staleness might have gone after this break, but Low still felt he needed a shake-up. With the promise of more space on the *Daily Herald*, and seeing the chance of working on the Labour paper as a new challenge, he resigned from the *Standard* at the end of 1949. Beaverbrook, who heard the news in Jamaica, was dismayed. Dating his reply 'Black Friday', he warned Low that the decision was 'a disaster. It is unnecessary and inadvisable. That's what I think of it. You will like Percy [Cudlipp, the *Herald*'s editor] and you won't like the TUC bosses any more than Percy himself, who is always in trouble with Bevin and Morrison – except at Election time. Don't forget your old firm. Yours ever, Beaverbrook.'[84] Low's departure was news worldwide.

108 'No change – with a difference', *Evening Standard*, 4 November 1948

Harry Truman's victory in the United States presidential election of 1948 came as a stunning surprise. He had succceded to the Presidency on Franklin Roosevelt's death in 1945 but had faced an unsympathetic Congress and had in no way emerged from the great man's shadow.

TROUBLE ABOUT ONE OF LOW'S MODELS

109 'Trouble about one of Low's models', *Daily Herald*, 2 February 1950

Low's most famous symbol at this time, the TUC carthorse, was regarded by many members of the Labour movement as liable to misinterpretation. Such ambiguity suited Low. For him, if not for the zealots at Transport House, humorous misunderstandings added to the effectiveness of the symbol.

Beaverbrook was right. No doubt Low felt confident about Cudlipp, having worked with him at the *Standard*. Naturally the *Herald* gave him a tremendous fanfare, and readers learnt that Low had 'Left Wing opinions' but would 'enjoy the freedom on which he has always insisted – whenever he thinks fit he will poke fun at Labour personalities and criticise official policy'.[85] The *Herald* was not actually owned by the Labour Party: fifty-one per cent of the shares belonged to Odhams Press. But political policy was decided by directors nominated by the TUC – in effect, therefore, by the Labour Party – and the editor used to have to report to the Party's annual Conference.

Low clocked in on 1 February 1950. 'Jolly good luck to you,' wrote the *Daily Express* editor Arthur Christiansen, one of the great Fleet Street figures of his time. 'I loved the last cartoon on the *Standard* – and rather hopelessly hope that the *Herald* ones won't be so good!'; adding, 'No; I withdraw that.'[86] Harold Laski thought Low would be worth fifty seats to Labour at the *Herald* in the forthcoming general election. Many others were not so sure. Some of the comments may have been snide: 'there was something in the Low of January which seems somehow missing

110 'This is the road', *Evening Standard*, 27 January 1950

One of Low's last cartoons before joining the *Daily Herald*. There was to be a general election on 23 February, and Low used his Micawber Churchill to score points during the campaign. Here R. A. Butler, one of the rising Conservative leaders, is squashed by a backward-looking Churchill, who faces a somnolent Lord Woolton. Low's original depiction of Churchill as Micawber, 'waiting for something to turn up' after his election defeat in 1945, caused outrage among Churchill loyalists.

WORLD CITIZEN

WORLD CITIZEN

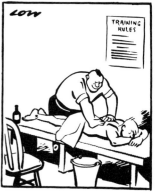

III World Citizen, *Daily Herald*, *c.* 1950s

Low invented and introduced to *Daily Herald* readers a postwar 'Common Man'. After a time he became 'World Citizen' and Low told of his adventures in strip form, once a week.

in the Low of February,' wrote the Tory *Spectator*. But Low quickly found that he was not settling in. His stock depiction of the TUC as 'an honest but simple-minded draught horse' ruffled feathers, and he did not find the readers as responsive as he hoped.[87]

Low's own mind was turning more and more towards issues transcending what he now thought of as the outmoded divisions of class and party. Nor did he find the new generation of political leaders so interesting to draw. From the 'Common Man', a bewildered character who cropped up in postwar cartoons, clad only in a trench coat, Low developed the idea of a strip cartoon about 'World Citizen', which would be syndicated around the world and reflect a world – not a British – view. The idea can be seen almost as a culmination: of his political ideas, focusing

"The motion is that we sheep and wolves promise never to attack one another, and to show we mean it we sheep will unconditionally stop wearing these dangerous bombs which might go off if anyone tried to bite us"

PEACE, IMPERFECT PEACE

(in a humorous way) on the plight of the citizen in a muddled world, 'banging up against the problem of living';[88] of the didactic streak which was now a larger part of his argumentative temperament; and of the technical possibilities for a worldwide audience that had excited him in 1928 when his cartoon was the first to be sent to North America by wireless.

The strip appeared weekly in the *Herald* from September 1951, in addition to his normal quota of cartoons. It was indeed syndicated around the world, but perhaps not as successfully as Low hoped, and it did not long survive.

★   ★   ★

112 'Peace, imperfect peace', *Daily Herald*, 1 November 1950

'Peace Conferences' of various kinds were a feature of Cold War propaganda in the postwar years. This one, sponsored by a 'World Peace Committee' in Prague and obviously Soviet-inspired, was to be held in Sheffield. When the British Government refused entry to delegates, Prague became the venue instead.

UNAVOIDABLE DEMANDS of REARMAMENT

Escape into Idealism

LOW

GONE WITH THE WIND

113 'Gone with the wind', *Daily Herald*, 24 April 1951

The Labour Government's programme of rearmament caused a major split in the party. When the Chancellor, Hugh Gaitskell, imposed Health Service charges to help pay for it, Aneurin Bevan, architect of the Service and leading opponent of the arms programme, resigned in protest. Gaitskell, Morrison, Shinwell and Dalton try to keep the party grounded in reality – as they (and Low) saw it.

'June 28th, 1952. Dear Mr Wadsworth, may I call and have a few words with you one day? I have an idea about my political cartoons which may interest you.' A. P. Wadsworth, editor of the *Manchester Guardian*, smartly said it would be a great delight; 'I will adapt myself to your convenience.' The convenience proved mutual. The two parties agreed much the same contract that had served Low since he joined the *Evening Standard*, and he planned to supplement the *Guardian*'s more modest salary 'by overseas syndications and a few well-placed commissions abroad'. He was to provide 'three political cartoons and one strip', with a minimum width of three columns and a depth of six inches. At £5,000 he was paid £500 less than Beaverbrook paid him in 1929.

LIVELY VICTIM

114 'Lively victim', *Manchester Guardian*, 19 February 1958

The first substantial postwar revival of Liberalism lost the Conservatives the Rochdale by-election in 1958. Lord Hailsham, as Conservative Party Chairman, was a vociferous critic of Liberal tactics: 'The unpleasant truth is that our candidate was beaten by a candidate from a party which has a name but no policy, except abuse of the other two parties, . . . no philosophy, no outlook, and no ideas.'

It was more than the editor and managing director but probably half what the *Herald* had paid him. Low's last *Herald* cartoon appeared on 31 October. He left for a trip to the Far East and started at the *Guardian* on 1 February.[89]

The *Guardian* (it dropped the 'Manchester' in 1959) was Low's harbour. It seems, in retrospect, the obvious postwar place: serious, progressive, the right platform for an argumentative cartoonist who liked his readers to think. His contract was renewed at three-yearly intervals and he never retired.

The paper was capable of ingenious blunders. 'When the Gaitskell [caricature] was returned to me the other day, I was horrified to find that the drawing had been mutilated by the cutting out with the scissors and re-fixing with tape of the title. This was done presumably to perform a second offence: as you know, drawings of heads tend to have a fatal sameness if one does not constantly strive for change. I drew Gaitskell with a slightly quizzical look, his head at an angle characteristic to his familiars.

THE RE-THINKER

115 'The re-thinker', *Manchester Guardian*, 13 October 1953

Labour was overrun in the general election of October 1959. The party suffered its third successive defeat and its worst result since the war. Obviously it was a time to rethink the party's position. Low shows Hugh Gaitskell starting to do so.

The Art Department decided to straighten it up, thereby losing my point and giving it the conventional appearance. What must I do to avoid such disasters in the future?'[90] But there is a respect, almost deference, in the editors' dealings, especially from the pen of the young editor who succeeded Wadsworth, Alastair Hetherington. That did not prevent firm editorial decisions about the placing of cartoons and their occasional 'holding over' when unsuitable. (Wadsworth to Low, of a cartoon about Churchill's relatives: '... I am sorry but I think it is a bit too obscure for our literal-minded public – without a dose of historical explanation'.)[91]

Low's biggest sensation on the *Guardian* was his own Corona-

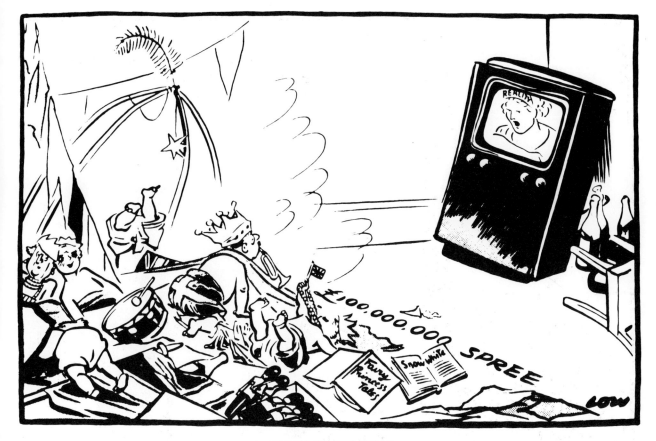

MORNING AFTER

tion fanfare in 1953. Published on 3 June, the day after the ceremony, and captioned 'Morning After', it was designed to bring people back to earth with a bump. 'I don't mind how unconventional you are!' Wadsworth had written in advance. He offered space in the Coronation Supplement too, but Low felt anything but a 'rather heavy allegorical piece might jar in such a setting'.[92]

The 'Morning after' jarred just like old times. It ricocheted round the world. Wadsworth did not see it coming and was writing 'What a mercy everything is over now!' even as readers penned their outrage. 'I certainly spoke too soon,' he resumed in his next letter. 'The letters began to pour in on Wednesday night . . . So far there are 126 anti-Low, which is of course less than 1 per 1,000 readers, but they are very widely spread.' The paper published a large selection and a leading article, which prompted more. The final total, including a dozen from overseas, was 383 against and 192 for.[93]

116 'Morning after', *Manchester Guardian*, 3 June 1953

By background and temperament, Low was perhaps less likely than most to fall prey to the euphoria of the Coronation and the dawn of a 'new Elizabethan age'. Even he may have been surprised at some of the readers' letters: 'lowest taste', 'unsuitably vulgar', 'Union Jack in the most insulting position on the human frame', 'repulsive', 'scandalous', 'a new low in sheer bad taste' . . .

Eliot was pleased to be included in *Low's Company* – but was surprised to find himself looking slightly like General de Gaulle.

T. S. Eliot

Low had meanwhile continued his portrait caricatures. The *Saturday Book*, an annual, published a dozen in 1945, eight of which were included among the fifty in *Low's Company* (1952), which had verses by Helen Spalding and L. A. G. Strong, and a bias towards 'the young'. 'What is one to say about a caricature of oneself?' asked T. S. Eliot. 'It is so extremely difficult for the victim to judge: but I am surprised to note a certain resemblance to General de Gaulle which I had never noticed before.' 'I will frankly declare I don't like it very much,' wrote J. B. Priestley. '. . . Can anything be done about it, apart from lightening the shading, or has it gone too far?' 'My wife . . . asked me to tell you that you are a truly great man because only you have been able to see me as I really am!' was Aneurin Bevan's comment.[94]

Many of the drawings in *Low's Company* were published first in the *Leader* magazine. Low's requests for sittings were of course

greeted as a compliment. Nigel Balchin, John Piper and David Lean were 'flattered' and Alec Guinness 'enchanted' as well. Hartley Shawcross, Barbara Ward and P. M. S. Blackett said it was an honour. Sir Gerald Kelly presented the original of himself to the Royal Academy, of which he was President. But when Evelyn Waugh discovered the portrait would appear in an album, he politely declined to sit: 'I should hate to appear in an album ... It was nice of you to think of including me among your "celebrities", but without me the Book of Beauty is losing nothing.'[95] The book was widely reviewed, as might be expected, and on the whole favourably.

Low drew caricatures occasionally for the *Guardian* too. He illustrated the serialisation of Winston Churchill's memoirs in the USA and drew a large cartoon for *Illustrated* to mark Churchill's eightieth birthday. He designed an inn sign for the Lord (Herbert) Morrison pub in Lambeth; and published two more anthologies, *Low Visibility* (1953) and *The Fearful Fifties* (1960), the latter of which included much more text than usual. *Low's Autobiography* (1956) was serialised in the *Evening Standard, Manchester Guardian, Life* and the *Bulletin*.

The autobiography has great verve; the product towards the end of his life of the old self-confidence. But although it was affectionately received, several reviewers considered it marred by com-

Canterbury

Within the cartoon: CHAIN REFLEYES · FRUSTRATION · REPRESSED IMPULSE · SUBCONSCIOUS · LIBIDO · COMPLEX · Adler · Jung · Freud

The Home Secretary is considering Sir R. Boothby's suggestion that a Royal Commission should review the laws relating to homosexuality.

LOW

WASHING DAY

120 'Washing day', *Manchester Guardian*, 23 February 1954

This cartoon generated another crop of irate letters. The Home Secretary, Sir David Maxwell-Fyfe (later Visc. Kilmuir) did indeed set up a Royal Commission which, under the chairmanship of Sir John Wolfenden, led to a relaxation of the law on sexual offences. Years before, when Low was attacking the dictators, Freud had written a postcard of appreciation, in heavy black ink: 'A Jewish refugee from Vienna, a very old man personally unknown to you, cannot resist the impulse to tell you how much he admires your glorious art and your inexorable, unfailing criticism.'

placency. Self-confidence had turned into what Stephen Potter called 'a certain cockiness, an I-was-rightness'. Paul Jennings had already detected a 'faint air of I-told-you-so' about *Low Visibility*, and the *Times Literary Supplement* was to find 'a slight tendency to be didactic and even governessy' in the *Fearful Fifties*.[96]

Bernard Shaw was one who criticised the autobiography for complacency. Shaw figures hardly at all in the book (except as a subject for caricature) yet is precisely the sort of man Low might have been expected to want to know. Possibly they did not click. Shaw thought the book deficient in charm: 'This is partly, I suppose, because it is a chronicle of almost unbroken professional success. The hard and critical temperament that made Low such a great cartoonist is not altogether lovable.' Shades of J. F. Archibald and Norman Lindsay, and the young man on the make.[97]

The predicament of the man who has been justified too often by events is familiar. Poor Low: was it such a fault? It may have been more noticeable for combining with a certain appearance

THE DARK HORSE

of self-importance in his later years. An artist who for a time had a studio in the same house found him 'very much the great man and *very* heavy' – not at all like the self-portraits. A *Guardian* reporter recalls the paper's arrangements for covering the annual party conferences (always big affairs) being very much orientated round Low. At a guest night at an Oxford college, Low and another distinguished guest each left the impression of vying to be treated as the guest of honour. What would the Low of the *Bulletin* have thought of the Low of 1962 accepting a knighthood? (He had turned one down in the 1930s.) The tribal chieftain in Low's anecdote would have had Low's head in a trice, one suspects. Poor Low again. For what may have seemed self-importance in the celebrity was more likely shyness, self-protection, the wish for privacy and consideration for family.

121 'The dark horse', *Manchester Guardian*, 3 July 1959

On 1 July the Belgian Government confirmed its decolonisation policy for the Congo, despite resistance from white settlers. Low uses Wimbledon as a topical metaphor. British Blimps are horrified at the thought of African independence – and Verwoerd (South Africa), Welensky (Central African Federation) and De Gaulle look disturbed.

WORKERS' COUNCIL

"NO HONOUR, NO PITY, NO HUMANITY?"
"NOTHING BUT **THIS**"

COMRADESHIP IN HUNGARY

122 'Comradeship in Hungary', *Manchester Guardian*, 12 December 1956

Kruschev sent Soviet tanks into Hungary while the world's attention was diverted by the invasion of Suez. The Hungarians, led by Imre Nagy, had been turning against Soviet Russia and moving towards a position of neutralism. The Russian response was uncompromising and brutal.

123 (opposite) 'The colossus of Suez', *Manchester Guardian*, 31 July 1956

Nasser nationalised the Suez Canal on 26 July 1956, starting a crisis that culminated in October–November in the Anglo–French–Israeli invasion. At this early stage, Low shared the general British hostility to Nasser's action and the fear that Russia would be the beneficiary.

124 (opposite) 'Above all, the little dear must not be frustrated', *Manchester Guardian*, 6 April 1956

Low reverts to a characteristic device, 'the child-mind', in this criticism of the consumer boom of the 1950s. Like many people of his generation, Low felt that too much material comfort would distract young people from the serious responsibilities of citizenship in a democracy.

THE COLOSSUS OF SUEZ

ABOVE ALL THE LITTLE DEAR MUST NOT BE FRUSTRATED

Even Low's intellectual combativeness and individualism might be mistaken for self-importance when he was famous. So might his ambition to cartoon for a worldwide audience and 'to contribute towards human understanding and the betterment of mankind'.[98]

Low's opinions were the product of his curiosity. When he had learnt about something, he expressed his views with conviction and skill. If the corollary in later life was an unwitting air of self-satisfaction, that was little enough for his public to pay.

Low had bouts of poor health in the last three years of his life. He continued at the *Guardian* until April 1963 and died on 19 September after several weeks in hospital.

II Low's Art

What did people think was so good about Low? Before he was fifty, his work was in major galleries. He was compared to Gillray and Rowlandson and was in a British Museum exhibition called, informally, 'Leonardo to Low'. William Rothenstein had called him one of the three great satirists of his time, alongside Shaw and Max Beerbohm. His colleague Strube, another celebrated cartoonist, said that he had made England 'a land fit for cartoonists to live in'. His success was not only, as Shaw said, 'largely unbroken'; it was also unchanging, in the sense that the qualities discerned in him varied very little with time and among critics. Partly this could be because his work gradually became the standard by which newspaper cartooning was judged. More probably, it was because his style matured early and changed little, making allowance for variations in space, printing and the type of newspaper for which he worked. The reviewer of *Low's Russian Sketchbook* in the *Bulletin* recalled that Low had learnt 'little or nothing on the technical side' after coming to the *Bulletin* from New Zealand, and judged from the *Sketchbook* that he had learnt little in the fourteen years since he left Australia either. 'He is Low, *sui generis*, unchanging and probably unchangeable; a phenomenon.'[1] Reactions when Low's work reached London were thus much the same as in Australia and continued the same. Even the almost apologetic criticisms after the Second World War were more to do with the subjects of his cartoons than his art; the aptness of events to the medium of the black-and-white artist seemed to have declined by comparison with the war and prewar years.

People were struck, almost literally from the *Big Budget* onwards, by Low's natural ability as a draughtsman. 'With such a gifted youth as Low, the drawing is ever the thing,' wrote an Australian commentator when he had been with the *Bulletin* a few years.[2] He had an extraordinary ability, also, to get to the nub of an issue. With corresponding skill he could capture a likeness. As Max Beerbohm acknowledged, he was a master of caricature. His cartoons were fresh, lively, humorous, witty. 'There is pep in Low's work,' the critic Frank Swinnerton wrote in 1921,

"PHEW! THAT'S A NASTY LEAK. THANK GOODNESS IT'S NOT AT OUR END OF THE BOAT."

125 'Phew! That's a nasty leak. Thank goodness it's not at our end of the boat', *Evening Standard*, 24 May 1932

This cartoon was widely reproduced around the world. Low recalled it much later with some satisfaction as 'boiling down a complicated situation to one point' (*New York Times*, 2 April 1961).

The world slump of 1929–32 left the economies of many countries in disarray. 'The pound and the dollar left the gold standard and the franc struggled to avoid devaluation. The British, United States and French governments were more concerned with their own immediate problems than with the trouble that was brewing for everybody at the other end of the boat.' (*Years of Wrath*, p. 9)

'a quality to which in English cartoons we are unaccustomed.' As well as humour, there was good humour – an absence of malice. 'He is not a savage hitter,' said the artist Paul Nash, 'but he is never afraid of hitting hard.'[3]

It is easy to be cavalier about natural skills; to assume that because they come naturally they need no work. But to be self-taught, like Low, is different from not learning at all. 'Low draws as the fishes swim,' said Arnold Bennett (proud, no doubt, of his reputation as the agent of Low's arrival in London). But Low did not like his skill brushed over. 'There is too much talk about the gift for drawing,' he told an interviewer. 'It is a capacity for work that gets you there.' Low once described how he traced over a Max caricature to see what the secret was. When one looked at the features and clothes, 'it was perfectly obvious that that was the right way to draw them, if only one could . . . but all I discovered was that the fellow who had done it could do it, and that I could not'.[4] The style of Phil May, Low discovered,

124

was similarly deceptive. The sureness of touch seemed spontaneous but was contrived. May worked on the *Bulletin* from 1886 to 1888 and had already returned to England, to *Punch*, before Low was born. Now he influenced Low's style, just as he influenced others in Australia. A hallmark obvious in many of Low's *Bulletin* drawings is the form of shading with parallel lines in the manner most easy to the hand, jocularly spoken of by artists, Low said, as 'the north-west system of line work'.

Low's line thus evolved through discipline and practice – and in this sense, unlike, say, Beerbohm's, it was not strictly 'natural' at all. Moreover, he habitually drew from models, not out of his head. Three features of his style evoked comment. There was, firstly, its fluency. Ronald Searle referred to 'something of an oriental facility in his handling of the brush'. 'I can think of only one other artist whose ink flows with such vitality,' commented Edmund Dulac in 1927, 'and that is Masayoshi, the Japanese. No doubt had he been born in the shadow of Fuji, Mr Low would have been renowned as a master of brushwork.'[5]

With fluency went an exquisite certainty and economy of line, belying the painstaking pencil sketch beneath it and rarely failing. If it occasionally seemed banal in later years, that was as much from familiarity, perhaps, as from declining powers. Low's cartoons never seemed fussy or cluttered. His powers of composition were masterly. He could group figures and objects with dramatic effect, through such favourite devices as the 'flying wedge' – of politicians, jackbooted soldiers, refugees or pigs. He used large contrasting masses of black ink and white space on a scale unprecedented in British newspapers, and he had to still the grumbles of the printers on the *Star* to do so. When he thought he was losing half-an-inch of column depth at the *Evening Standard* his complaint to the editor was not from simple pique. His placing of individual figures within the overall design was precise. 'Every cartoon is a puzzle, a kind of plot to ensure that the eye of the viewer is drawn first to one point, then to another in a regular sequence up to a climax, when the full idea is brought out. The success of the cartoon depends upon the viewer unconsciously picking up these points in the right sequence.'[6] Individual figures themselves are posed with great thought to what now would be called 'body language' – the nuances attached to the bend of an arm, the tilt of a head.

Low, in sum, worked on his natural ability, refined it, and adapted it superbly to his purposes. 'I started out to be a comic artist. Curiosity to find out how the wheels went around led me to the

Among Low's unpublished papers is a detailed account of the meticulous way in which he built up his portrait caricatures. He takes the example of Bernard Shaw. First Low sketches Shaw giving a lecture. He views him from various positions ('We will not delude ourselves that we can understand an object by looking at one side of it'). He jots down notes of general impressions ('twinkling', 'bouncy') that are still too undefined to put into drawing.

'Now we go home – but not to work seriously on Shaw for a few days. In spare moments, between other jobs, we flick off odd little sketches from our stored-up memories of him.

'We now apply to Shaw for a personal sitting. (Naturally, he consents.)' On this occasion the sketches will be 'tighter' and more detailed, and Low pays special attention to 'the action of Shaw's eyes and mouth' and to his movements.

'After this we go and draw our caricature.' The notes are abandoned, except for checking details. Three-quarter profile or full-face is best, since 'both eyes may be given their true value in relation to the rest of the face.

'The figure is blocked in large, filling the space available and leaving but little margin at top and bottom, to hint at towering personality. The head is cocked a trifle on one side to bring out a certain roguishness. The chest is thrown out a little to convey "bounce". We must have that hand on the hip, characteristic of the platform Shaw, but we will also hint that there still survives a little self-conscious Shaw inside that has to fumble at his coat-button. The face is drawn in from the face already drawn in our minds. The head now comes with its length accentuated naturally; the whiskers are now more controversial. We remember little lines over the eye-brows which give him a certain quizzical look. Two small wrinkles at the corner of the near eye, a touching-up of the whiskers round the corner of the mouth to suggest the line that must come underneath whenever Shaw smiles: these bring him to the required degree of happiness. A few soft smears of pencil across the nose and cheeks add something to this also. They suggest a pinkness and an "Irishness". We "feel" under the beard for the chin so that the set of the mouth may be right. That lip and the two teeth – they practically draw themselves. Now with a half-tone line on the right side of the forehead we suggest the dome-like shape of its appearance in profile. Although a half-tone line, yet a most important one. A blacker pencil to lay in a few heavier "spots" to give body. A rubber to rub away the labour which is too evident, to shorten and disconnect lines to give an effect of careless ease in draughtmanship.'

A famous toreador has publicly offered to teach Bernard Shaw bull-fighting. Of course Shaw being a vegetarian, a carrot would be substituted for the bull.

127 Low's Topical Budget (detail), *Evening Standard*, 30 March 1935

Shaw cartooned rather than caricatured.

world of ideas and I became a graphic satirist. Circumstances made me a political caricaturist.'[7]

Low's ability to see beyond the end of his political nose, as Anthony Blunt put it, accounted for the sharpness of his cartoon comments.[8] The matching skill at catching character made him an outstanding caricaturist. Good cartooning and good caricature do not necessarily go together, and they were certainly an uncommon combination in the Fleet Street of Low's time. Low dwelt at length on the relation between the two. 'The aim of the caricaturist', he stated in *Ye Madde Designer*, 'is to discover, analyse and select essentials of personality, and by the exercise of wit to reduce them to appropriate form.' A cartoon, by contrast, was not a type of draughtsmanship but 'an illustration of a political or social idea, served up sometimes in caricatural draughtsmanship, sometimes not.' Getting the right idea for a cartoon was thus at least half the battle. 'There are few in whom the ability to draw,' Low noted, 'is accompanied by the ability to appreciate the significance of events.'[9]

There can be no doubt that Low was very perceptive about politics. His writings and his success as a wartime broadcaster show how good he was also in distilling the apt comment from a brew

127

SCIENTIFIC RESEARCH AT THE NATIONAL LABORATORIES.

128 'Scientific research at the national laboratories', *Evening Standard*, 8 January 1934

Low chides Hilton Young, Minister of Health in the National Government, for doing 'research' instead of acting directly on the problem of slum clearance and public health.

The 'body language' of the individual figures is most expressive, and the three groups are skilfully composed to draw the eye to the different parts of the design. The 'unemployed stomach' in the top corner is a characteristic piece of Low frivolity.

of events. He was, for a cartoonist, very wordy. In addition to a caption, his cartoons often have fifty words or more within the frame. It is part of his 'argumentative' style. Colonel Blimp, his best known symbol, is only a vehicle for verbal comment: indeed he could almost be said to resemble a 'voice bubble' which has taken on the shape of its speaker.

Low's apt comments made sense, moreover, to the millions. One of the many problems of working in a period of mass circulations (still rapidly developing when Low came to London) was the need, as he used unflatteringly to put it, 'to circumscribe oneself by the intelligence of the bonehead'.[10] Low had the ability to make people think they saw instantly what he was getting at. Whether they were right, and how far they all saw the same thing, was a different matter; and many of the rows about his cartoons turned, of course, upon mistakes about his intentions. ('I am astonished at what goes on inside the heads of my customers sometimes. The simplest idea is liable to be picked up in all kinds of different ways by different people.')[11] Whatever the meaning attached,

BLIMP IN CYPRUS

129 'Blimp in Cyprus', *Manchester Guardian*, 29 August 1956

The occasion is particular – on/off negotiations with Archbishop Makarios over the future of Cyprus. The Blimps are general and traditional – their inane words capable of application to a wide range of die-hard reaction.

Low's cartoons carried to his readers a great strength of conviction. 'I have looked often on his cartoons,' bewailed the popular journalist A. J. Cummings, 'with the envious admiration of one who sees the laborious argument of a thousand words impressed on the page in the few fatal strokes of an incomparable artist.'[12]

Those fatal strokes employed the graphic imagery of what E. H. Gombrich calls 'the cartoonist's armoury'.[13] Much of Low's freshness came from his original and inventive use of symbols. The creation of new symbols, he emphasised, was no easy matter, 'for a good cartoon is fifty per cent suggestion, dotted with half-ideas to be completed with the unconscious cooperation of the person who looks at it'. While new symbols might seem obscure, the danger with old ones was that they drugged the mind instead of stimulating it.[14]

Low could not avoid familiar symbols altogether. He used plenty of John Bulls in his settling-in period at the *Star*, for instance. But he constantly strove to get beyond them. Joan Bull displaced John. His allegorical Britannia and Peace figures were

MICAWBER MINISTRY

130 'Micawber ministry',
Manchester Guardian, 14 January 1958

A typical use of the cartoonist's habit of literary analogy. Low extends the Micawber comparison, previously limited to Winston Churchill in opposition after 1945, to include an entire group of senior Conservative Ministers – Amory, Butler, Lloyd, Macleod and Hailsham. Hailsham's handbell became a tab of identity after he roused the Conservative Party Annual Conference by wielding it on the rostrum.

creatures of flesh and blood. He used the conventional weapons, too, of literary, historical and artistic analogy. His artistry gave them an extended life, so that his Micawber Churchill, say, waiting for something to turn up after 1945, could become a running joke.

The cartoons in this book illustrate amply too Low's use of the cartoonist's various other weapons. Politicians become animals and are put in all kinds of incongruous guises. Topical events – games of cricket, horse races, plays – become metaphors for politics. Familiar verbal images are given graphic form: shipwrecks, battlefields, storms. Ideas are driven home by the exaggeration of figures and by contrasts in scale.

All such devices are the cartoonist's stock-in-trade. Low used them skilfully. But perhaps his most distinctive skill was to overcome the problem of creating new symbols and to bring the likes

FRONT ROW (left to right)

SPIRIT OF LOYALTY, FIELD-MARSHAL PIP-SQUEAK CHURCHILL (wearing his old man's hat) WITH STAFF SQUIBS, MUNITIONS TRANSPORT. BOER WAR VETERANS.
IN CHAR-A-BANC, LETTER-WRITERS TO EDITORS, STATUES OF PAST PRESIDENTS OF THE UNION, BRITANNIA (recovering from puncture).

ON TO THE NEW PRIDE'S PURGE AT OXFORD.

131 'On to the new pride's purge at Oxford', unpublished, *c.* 1933

This drawing (too strong to publish?) is crowded with stock devices of the cartoonist's trade – flags, national symbols, stereotype figures, all in a grand marchpast. The occasion was a notorious Oxford Union debate in February 1933 when undergraduates voted against fighting 'for King and Country'. Low pictures outraged citizens rallying behind Winston Churchill's son Randolph (see detail), who had jumped onto the jingoistic bandwagon. Blimp was not yet invented, otherwise he would doubtless have been in the van. Note that Low misspells 'battalion'. Concentration on drawing meant that spelling mistakes quite often slipped in.

LOW'S ANNUAL PARTY FOR HIS MODELS

1 Spirit of the New Year.
2 Hailé Selassie.
3 Peace, Justice, Civilization and What-not.
4 Golden Calf with the Banks up.
5 The Arts.
6 Mrs Fantail, Low's charlady.
7 Upanupanup and Onanonanon.
8 Lord Beaverbrook disguised as Low
9 Joan Bull repelling suitors.
10 Musso.
11 Oyeh Sezu, Japanese correspondent
12 Mrs Wowser and Depression
13 Spirit of Czarism and Lucy Houston.

of Blimp before the world. The list of his characters across the years is extremely rich, even if many had comparatively short lives. There were the Coalition Ass, Joan Bull, Onanonanon and Upanupanup, Colonel Blimp, Oyeh Sezu, Calamity Yowl, the TUC carthorse, the Common Man, and the World Citizen, amongst others.

The origins and success of the Ass were described in Chapter I. The animal had great verve, possibly because it was an image of inherent tension. It was mobile, springy, alert, expressive. It would have been fun to play with a toy one. Its eyes, set in ovals of white space, were especially expressive and it had four of them. It could act almost as a double image, like twins, a Siamese Tweedledum and Tweedledee; either in unison, each head identical, or in contrast – one head with ears up, the other ears down.

In itself, then, the Ass was a very flexible visual symbol – rather in contrast to Blimp. Its meaning too remained precise, whereas Low lost control of Blimp. The Ass fitted exactly the condition of the Coalition Government between 1918 and 1922, when

132 (opposite) 'Low's annual party for his models', *Evening Standard*, 28 December 1935

An end-of-year celebration amply illustrating Low's claim to have 'invented' his times and his cast of characters. Among the inventions are Sir John Simon, Ramsay MacDonald and Stanley Baldwin. French Premier Pierre Laval vies with Hitler for Joan Bull's embrace. Note also the characters Oyeh Sezu, Upanupanup and Onanonanon.

THE ARGUMENT

A difference of opinion as to the direction of the winning-post

133 'The argument', *Star*, c. 1920

Low's Ass was a highly adaptable symbol. Tensions between its two ends often provided the meat of a cartoon.

A HEAD TOO MANY
'If I only knew which half to drown!'

134 'A head too many', *Star*, *c.* 1920

Low put the Ass into all sorts of predicaments. Here Lloyd George has to make a calculation of electoral advantage: should he favour the Liberal or the Conservative end of his Coalition Government?

Lloyd George and his Cabinet were sustained by two parties which, but for the war, would not have coalesced in the first place and now hesitated to break up only for fear of the consequences. The two parties could work to the same end yet at any moment might break out in a flurry of snapping and snarling.

The possibilities for the Ass were endless. It could be the butt of the cartoon joke, either because of the relation of its two parts (it stands on a weighing machine after a by-election to test its Liberal end, for instance) or because of something done to it. It is threatened by a buzz-saw in a Victorian melodrama and with a new spine by Churchill and Birkenhead. It is fed a monotonous diet of broken pledges. In particular, of course, its relationship with Lloyd George provided great scope. The Ass carries Lloyd George as jockey and acrobat, dances to his bagpipes, pulls his barrow, dresses up as his reindeer. At other times the Ass could point up or reinforce the joke, if Lloyd George himself were the

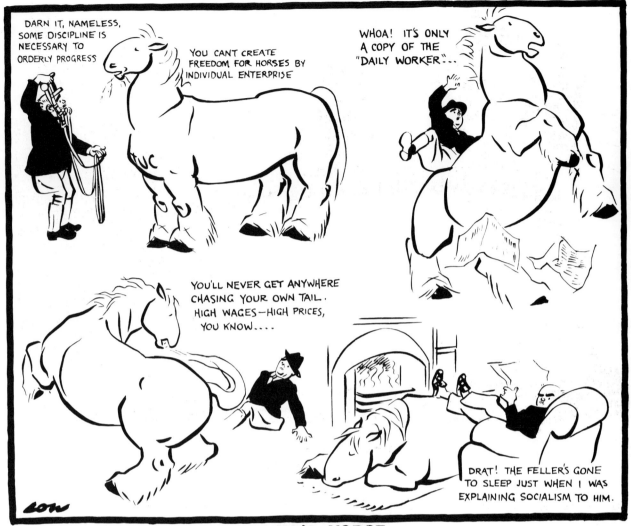

LOW'S HORSE

main butt. In that role, it rides a tank with him, climbs trees and ladders, plays cricket and forms part of the Laocoon statue. Low said he took a little time to work out the basic design of the creature, but 'after that I could have drawn him with my eyes shut'.[15]

The TUC carthorse served Low in much the same way, though with less flexibility. Again the symbol was precise. The idea of organised Labour as 'an honest but simple-minded draught horse' is unlikely to have been original. It had featured in Low's own work by the time he left Australia, and it cropped up almost immediately in the *Star*. Only after the 1945 general election, however, did the horse come into its own and carry a TUC label. Although Low from time to time protested in print that such

135 'Low's horse', *Evening Standard*, 8 May 1946

Low refused to name his TUC carthorse. When a newspaper competition was organised, Low was unimpressed. He said 'The horse is a dear old thing, with a noble past and probably a glorious future. I refuse to give him a rude or inept name' (*Evening Standard*, 24 April 1946).

horses are sturdy, strong, kindly creatures, it was not surprising that the symbol caused trouble with union leaders. Low intimates that this was even a factor in his decision to leave the *Daily Herald*.[16]

Blimp's natural history has already been told. Low determined on his personality, appropriately enough for a symbol whose force consisted chiefly in what he said, before choosing his physical form. 'I decided to invent a "character" typifying the current disposition to mixed-up thinking, to having it both ways, to dogmatic doubleness, to paradox and plain self-contradiction.' The form was chosen when he visited a Turkish bath for a 'Low and Terry' feature and overheard 'two pink sweating chaps of military bearing' in a blimpish conversation. He had just read, too, a letter in the papers from 'some Colonel or other' saying that cavalry should continue to wear their traditional uniform and spurs even when they were mechanised. So '*Colonel* Blimp, of course!'[17]

Blimp's home was a single-frame pocket cartoon in the Topical Budget. Low's delight in the humour of word play had full rein. Some of Blimp's aphorisms were genuine paradoxes whose suitability as a basis for policy was a matter of argument, and which

136 'Resolved by Blimp', Topical Budget (detail), *Evening Standard*, 1 January 1938

GAD, GENTLEMEN, HERE'S TO OUR GREATEST VICTORY OF THE WAR

Low thought plainly absurd: 'The Tory Party must save the Empire if it has to strangle it in the attempt' (the logic of nuclear arms is precisely comparable). 'Hitler only needs arms so that he can declare peace on the rest of the world' (this, again, can be read as a statement of the balance of power principle). Other aphorisms became unself-contradictory if metaphors were unmixed, negatives removed or extra steps inserted in the argument: 'If we want to keep our place in the sun, we must darken the sky with our airplanes.' 'War is NOT inevitable and it never will be unless we do something about it.' Others are just blather and word play: 'Bayonets bring out the best in a man – and it stays out.' 'The League of Nations is a big sham. Why, it's nearly all foreigners.'

When Blimp moved into the big weekday cartoons, he was used like Low's other symbols. Sometimes blimpish attitudes were the main point; sometimes his presence labelled specific people as blimpish, through guilt by association. Low multiplied him at will. A single cartoon might be full of Blimps. Blimp also appeared in a variety of dress, though most often he just wore

137 'Gad, gentlemen, here's to our greatest victory of the war', *Evening Standard*, 10 January 1940

In a ghastly parody of some regimental rite, army Blimps toast the removal of Hore-Belisha from the War Ministry. Neville Chamberlain serves as waiter. Low rams home his criticism by a rigid, repetitive composition. He takes care, too, in attacks such as this one, not to include himself in the frame. Instead a drunken goat here emphasises his contempt.

his bath towel. By late 1942 Low calculated that Blimp had made more than 260 appearances, which he categorized as follows:

Military virtues (and vices)	7
Feudal–aristocratic tradition	3
Home and Empire policy	69
Foreign policy	139
Miscellaneous	47

As a cartoon symbol Blimp was thus fairly adaptable. Nakedness – and the anonymity of a Turkish bath – detached him from too specific an environment and made it easier for Low to claim that he was criticising all and every stupidity: 'Not of Colonels, nor of stupid Colonels in particular. Not of Authority, nor especially of stupid Authority. Not exclusively of the Right Wing nor the Left. Stupidity has no frontiers, domestic or foreign, party, professional or social.'[18] Rotundity has often been associated, in modern Britain at least, with complacency, flatulence and sloth of mind – alike in Gillray's Prince Regent, Dickens' Fat Boy, Billy Bunter and the stereotyped capitalist. The walrus moustache was a splendid tab of identity, adding an animal touch and helping further to create a visual image to deflate the verbal message. (At least once a Blimp head is fixed to a bulldog's body.) The 'Colonel' prefix helped to set Blimp up but was actually a limitation. It made the depiction of left-wing stupidity more difficult; a problem which the invention of 'Pmilb', Blimp's left-wing brother who stood on his head, did not satisfactorily solve. 'Bishop Blimp' or 'Dr Blimp', which Low considered as alternatives, would have been equally limiting.

Blimp's very success was a problem for Low. When a symbol becomes public property, a cartoonist cannot use it with certainty to convey a precise meaning. As a verbal device, Blimp was easily imitated. People, including friends, wrote to Low adopting Blimp's style ('Gad, Sir! This can't go on'). Few people, of course, ever had the temerity to send him drawings of his graphic symbols. All who wished could imitate Blimp, where few could imitate the Ass or the Carthorse. More important, Blimp's reference was so wide – 'stupidity' – that people could read it how they wished. Like 'freedom' or 'justice', the argument could be as much about recognising it in practice as defining it in the abstract.

A Blimp cartoon had several layers of meaning. Blimp's own remarks generally contained at least two, because of the element

138 'Diehard mentality', *Star*, 8 April 1927

These two 'diehard dimwits' from the *Star* clearly anticipate the Colonel Blimp of seven years later. In 1934 Low would match their verbal mannerisms with the bloated physiques he had spotted in the Australian Turkish baths (see Fig. 60).

DIEHARD MENTALITY

of paradox or contradiction. In the pocket cartoons, further, Low was an enigmatic listener, to whom could be attributed an opposing view. Or did Low agree? What was he thinking, in or out of the picture? Low decided, after several years of watching widely varying reactions to Blimp, that there were three rough categories. Some people believed Blimp was a destructive representation of something bad and was therefore to be approved. Some thought him a destructive misrepresentation of something good, and therefore to be disapproved. Others again thought him a misrepresentation that was intended to be destructive but backfired on the artist because the misrepresentation only proved its goodness.[19] Low had fun with Blimp and was still using him as late as the 1959 general election. But Blimp had his tiresome side, and one can see how, like Conan Doyle with Sherlock Holmes, Low became bored with him.

The success of Low's symbols in conveying his meanings should not obscure the fact that the central element in his cartooning technique was the use of personal caricature. This included the caricature of himself. Opinions differed about how true to life was the artist's cartoon image, whether harangued by Blimp, escorting Joan Bull or got up in a barrel as Diogenes Low for the 1945 general election. In general, people found the real Low rather tougher and less startled or harassed in appearance.[20]

The formal definition quoted earlier – that cartoons are 'sometimes in caricatural draughtsmanship, sometimes not' – certainly needs amending for Low. In his case, it was *rarely* not. He continually identified policies and attitudes with persons who appeared to represent them: 'The person is merely the symbol of an idea.' This was the root of his admiration for Gillray, the man who 'closed the age of heavy Hogarthian generalisations'. 'With Gillray we see developing the familiar technique of our times – the selection of "characters" and their establishment as regular butts to be represented over and over again in different shapes and images of fantasy.'[21]

Low dismissed the portraits in newspaper cartoons as bearing little real likeness to the persons they stood for. Even so, there were gradations of likeness. There might be a generalised version, such as Low's Billy Hughes ('"Billy" was my own property'), or Lloyd George. No other cartoonist got under Lloyd George's skin so skilfully as Low, commented the *Nation and Athenaeum*; *Punch* cartoons, by contrast, 'like photographs, more resemble the outer appearance'.[22]

Secondly there might be a cartoon likeness conveyed mainly by a few 'tabs of identity'. Low's Beaverbrook relied much on 'the smile'; his Herbert Morrison, on the quiff. 'Mr Baldwin without his pipe would be as pointless as King Charles without his spaniel,' wrote a reviewer. Among the Nazis, Low would have preferred Goebbels to be the leader. 'Hitler has the will to be picturesque . . ., but whatever you do with his face, his physiognomy is essentially weak to draw.' The toothbrush moustache and the forelock were tabs that solved the problem (not just for Low, of course).[23]

Beyond this, the tabs might virtually envelop a personality. Low used Neville Chamberlain's umbrella as a tab to symbolise his well-meant but hopelessly inadequate approach to halting the dictators. Eventually he caricatured Chamberlain *as* an umbrella.

THE KINDNESS OF THE CARTOONIST.

The Labour leader Jimmy Thomas dolled himself up in tails as a member of the first Labour Government. Low turned him into 'the Right Hon. Dress Suit, wearing his Jimmy Thomas'. Thomas' colleague George Lansbury said he could not look at him any more without seeing the Right Hon. Dress Suit.[24] (Low regretted the reduced scope for cartoonists in the declining variations in male dress after the 1930s.)

Low thus set up a balance, almost a tension, between the 'real' person and the cartoon image; the latter seeking by caricature to express the cartoonist's views about the person. The images might coincide or lie far apart. At one extreme, people recognised themselves in Low's cartoons with approval. At the other, Low enjoyed teasing his public that the cartoon image was real and the real person a fabrication – that he drew likenesses, as he often said, 'more like men than they are themselves'. 'Low had to invent a wide variety of imaginary characters to express himself in his cartoons,' he wrote in his 'auto-obituary'. 'Among the most notable were Lloyd George, Winston Churchill, Ramsay Mac-Donald, J. H. Thomas and Lord Beaverbrook, which were freely

139 'The kindness of the cartoonist', *Evening Standard*, late 1920s

'Thomas was a friendly soul and I saw him often. "I will hand you down to posterity, Jimmy," I said to him. "You don't 'and me down to posterity, David; you 'ound me down," says he. While my mail filled with angry letters from readers accusing me of gross assault on Thomas's dignity, there were very few cartoons about him that were not followed by an appreciative note next morning to "dear David" from "J.T."' (*Autobiography*, p. 186). The dress suit passed into the common currency and was soon used by other cartoonists.

imitated at the time of their appearance by persons claiming to be the originals.'[25]

A less extravagant version of that joke was the simple claim that Low 'does not have to bother to make the drawings like the man. The man begins to look like the drawings.'[26] How far Low really believed this – of Sir William Joynson-Hicks ('Jix'), a favourite target as Home Secretary, for example, or Herbert Morrison, a great fan – is difficult to judge. He was well aware of the value of the cartoonist to an ambitious politician ('. . . it pays to advertise') and was constantly flattered with their attentions. There was no such thing in the days of mass democracy, he argued, as a cartoonist's 'victim'. Politicians are always alert to their public reputation, so the claim may well have some justification. *Ye Madde Designer* is littered with anecdotes such as Austen Chamberlain, famous for his monocle, asking Low if he need wear it for a sitting, as he could not see with it very well.

Some people may have been content merely to let the cartoon image follow a life of its own. Ellen Wilkinson, MP, thought Beaverbrook, for one, enjoyed 'a curious popularity among people who have never met him and who hate his policies, simply because of the joky little imp into which Low has made him'.[27] How far in general the 'real' and the cartoon images used to coincide, and which of them (if either) moved towards the other, is another imponderable. In any case, Low provided for his mass audience one of the means through which they could form their opinions of public persons, alongside photographs and what they read – but not, until well after 1945, what they heard on radio or TV from the lips of the persons themselves.

To Low, the use of caricature in this way as a vehicle for conveying ideas was increasingly important. At the best of times the weakness of democracy, as he phrased it with typical pith, is that 'you always have to keep telling it what it is'. Symbolising policies in persons was the best way of getting ideas across to the greatest number.[28]

But a more particular reason for cartooning personalities in the mid-1930s, when the implications of mass circulation and mass democracy were both preoccupying Low, was the prominence of international issues. Low felt that the audience for these was more like-minded. More important, the Fascist dictatorships ruled anyway through leaders and leadership more than ideas. They played the cartoonists' own game. 'Ideas, if they are good ideas, are, after all, impervious to ridicule . . . But it is different with Personalities. No human being is perfect . . . The Leader who sets

MUSSOLINI
THE EMPEROR OF
THE MEDITERRANEAN

MUSSOLINI
THE GHASTLY FLOP

THE DREAM AND THE NIGHTMARE

himself up as a god is, so to speak, asking for it. He must protect himself from the criticism of the grin.'[29]

Whatever the nuances of the relationship between personality and appearance in cartoon images, they were infinitely more subtle in Low's portrait caricatures. Low took these extremely seriously, not only in the preparation and care of their execution and for the boost they might initially give to his career, but also in his claims for caricature as an art. He did not want to press these claims too far, so he sometimes forestalled protest by telling a joke about a Viennese pastry cook. This cook believed there were only three really serious arts in the world – sculpture, architecture and pastry-making. Of these, the greatest was undoubtedly pastry-making.[30]

Low called caricature the art of 'all-in' portraiture, of fusing together the physical and the spiritual, 'to show not Smith but his quality, to lose him in his own Smithness'. He elaborates his

140 'The dream and the nightmare', *Evening Standard*, 11 June 1940

Would Mussolini enter the war? Low catches the two extremes of personality of a leader who had strutted the stage since the early 1920s.

ideas and his technique in *Ye Madde Designer*: 'A complete likeness of an individual is only possible through the synthesis of what is seen and what is apprehended by other senses.' Thus the medieval artist who insisted on kissing his models to get their 'taste' was perfectly justified in artistic terms. Similarly the search for character may entitle the caricaturist to depict 'physical features and attributes which have no justification in material fact, but which suggest abstract qualities that could not otherwise be made plain'. Pointless exaggeration, on the other hand, is bad caricature: 'To draw big feet on a person whose feet have no tendency to bigness, and whose soul possesses no attribute which might be helped to outward expression by enlargement of his feet, is not to exaggerate, but to invent. The drawing of the feet is without any basis of truth and is not expressive of character.'[31]

Low's claim for caricature as 'serious' art lay in this all-in quality. The ordinary portrait painter worked to different conventions. Colour, composition, a stricter attention to physical proportion and likeness, might all constrain him. Surely we got a much better impression of the characters of Fox, Pitt and George III from the caricatures of Gillray, Low argued, than from their formal portraits. 'Never seen the portrait painter that could caricature,' he jotted in his notes. 'Reynolds – a little.' A portrait painter might rejoin that he is not concerned exclusively with character. But if character is the aim, Low's point has force. 'With all deference to portraitists of the graver sort it may fairly be said that the sketch of Mr [Arnold] Bennett will tell posterity something about him which it is unlikely to learn elsewhere,' commented John Rothenstein on Low's *New Statesman* drawing. 'The features in the sketch hardly resemble those of Mr Bennett; and that is perhaps the most remarkable thing about it.'[32]

Yet despite this willingness to invent and exaggerate, Low's caricatures take no great liberties with personal appearance. He is firmly in the British tradition of portrait caricature or the *portrait chargé*, from Robert Dighton through Pellegrini, Ward and others in *Vanity Fair* and its imitators, to Max Beerbohm and Low's contemporaries such as Powys Evans and Kapp. Apart from some exaggeration in stature – for example Keynes, Simon and Reith are elongated, Beaverbrook and Conrad are reduced, Belloc, Chesterton and Bevin are enlarged – Low achieved his effects through minute attention to details of expression and posture. Nor do the portrait caricatures have any great point to make beyond the expression of character. They are enlivened with wit, to be sure ('perhaps the first essential of caricature is that it should be

144

141 Arnold Bennett, *New Statesman*, first series 1926

Although Bennett was instrumental in bringing Low to England, the two men were never close. After their first meeting, Low observed: 'White quiff, pinkish face, heavy supercilious eyes, loose mouth, lumpy receding chin, streaky moustache, chesty carriage, a couple of stone weight more than he should be, neat little hands and feet. Striped suit, the famous fob. Fancy having a watch ticking there, I thought. He didn't look well. Stomach trouble.' (*Autobiography*, p. 113)

a lark'); and the interpretation of character itself constitutes a comment. But they do not aim to destroy, nor to point a moral.

This conception of caricature depends for success upon familiarity with the subject, primarily by the artist but by his public too if success is complete. The caricatures of Max Beerbohm, Low thought, were almost too much of a private joke between intimates to be accessible to people who did not share his acquaintance: 'Caricatures of Gentlemen, for Gentlemen, by a Gentleman.' (John Rothenstein called them, similarly, 'almost soliloquies'.)[33] Equally, Low criticised his own Australian caricatures (those, at least, which he did *en route* round the continent) as betraying superficiality of acquaintance with their subjects. The same criticism might be laid against some of the drawings in the last volume of caricatures, *Low's Company*. Some people, too,

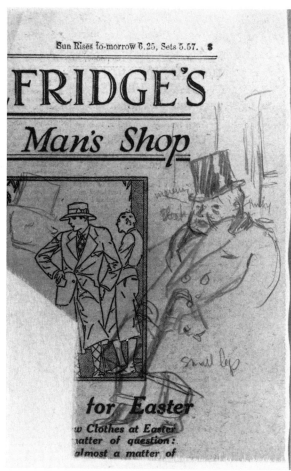

The Lord Chief Justice

FRIDGE'S Man's Shop for Easter

142 & 143 The Lord Chief Justice (Lord Hewart), *New Statesman*, first series 1926, and sketch for this

'Happy chance fixed things much better than I could have done, by bringing us together without pre-arrangement in an otherwise empty Underground railway carriage travelling to Golders Green at one o'clock in the morning. I was thunder-struck when the Lord Chief Justice of England, short, portly, tailed and top-hatted, evidently fresh from a party, got in at Leicester Square to pose for me. He did not know it, of course, but he must have wondered what the fellow over the way was up to so industriously behind his newspaper.' (*Autobiography*, pp. 136–37)

were simply difficult to know. Low found Attlee difficult – and Attlee was a notoriously uncommunicative person.

If the two *New Statesman* series are Low's most successful pub-lished caricatures, they are so perhaps because they were of people with a public reputation among the likely audience and who Low was ready to stalk and watch and study, at public meetings, din-ners, the Houses of Parliament – even on the Tube, where he quickly sketched the Lord Chief Justice, from whom he had little hope of a formal sitting. Formal sittings were sandwiched among these other occasions of scrutiny.

Low was habitually described in terms that slide into each other: lively, witty, humorous, sharp. He had a fine sense of the ridiculous, which he used to define as a clear perception of what *is*, contrasted with what *could be*.[34] He did not expect everyone to find him funny, for 'one man's humour will always be another man's silliness'. One reviewer of *Low's Political Parade* wrote 'Low is seldom funny', and another wrote 'Laughter is Low's chief weapon'. In general, obviously, he was in tune with the sense of humour of his readers. It was different in details from Australian humour, which was more American, he felt in 1919. But he had little difficulty adapting. Some of the initial attributions of 'liveliness', indeed, were a British response to the very directness and cheek of Australian humour, the 'larrikin' quality supposedly derived from the convict and Irish strain in Australian history.

Much of the liveliness was expressed through Low's skills of draughtsmanship. A telling phrase, often used, was that he liked to capture his subjects 'on the wing'. 'It is only when the subject is in movement that he betrays characteristic mannerisms and expressions.'[35] It would have been pointless asking Lloyd George to *sit* for him. The white locks and the features would all be there, 'but the something it is necessary to capture is the whatever-it-is that moves the outfit about.'[36] The Canterbury art school was so dreary because, while Low was interested in the Quick, 'what I did there belongs rather to the Dead. Very Still-life, anyway.' In the sort of testimonial the school could have done without, Low wrote (in response to criticism, not in gratuitous insult) that he had found no use in twenty years for anything he learned there.[37]

Low also maintained freshness by ringing the changes on his cartoon caricatures. 'Low draws a face for each successive cartoon as if he had never drawn it before . . .' noted the *Observer*. '[His caricatures] evolve and change with their subjects. "The Mr Baldwin of yesterday's cartoon will not do for the Mr Baldwin of today's."' That was written in 1927, perhaps with a dash of poetic licence.[38] In 13,000 cartoons (Low's own estimate in 1961), Low was bound to develop stock situations; while the very notion of tabs of identity, for example, defines limits to the cartoonist's range. Some of the small Blimp-and-Low drawings were used more than once with different captions. But bearing in mind that kind of detail, Low's variety is remarkable.

The liveliness came also from Low's ideas. He liked the definition of wit in cartoons as 'a propriety of thoughts and lines' or 'the juxtaposition of incongruous ideas'. Humour arose, rather, from incongruous circumstances: 'Humour is more of the earth, wit more of the spirit . . .'[39] In making such juxtapositions Low had an exceptionally good ear and quick eye. He enjoyed conundrums on the model of the 'more like you than you are' quotation earlier in this chapter. He liked to turn things round: 'Bomb severely damaged in Fleet Street'; 'South Korea kicked North

Korea on the boot with the seat of its pants'. Keynes, hoisting
the umbrella of 'anti-slump precautions', is accused by Blimp of
encouraging rain. Low was a gifted punster, as many of the
illustrations in this book will show.

Low's objectives as a cartoonist provided in themselves an
impetus for sharpness and wit. Caricature without purpose, he
argued, was mere comic art. '. . . If a caricaturist has any duty
to his fellow men other than to throw ripe tomatoes at them,
that duty is to lampoon stupidity where he finds it, and damn
the consequences.' Put more subtly, he believed that the most
important caricature and cartoon is satirical, 'and satire is essentially an art of complaint and disapproval, its best effects being
most readily produced in the spirit of opposition'. Its effectiveness
has therefore to be gauged as much by negative reactions as by
positive. Caricature should be the critic of the social system, not
its servant.[40]

These beliefs were reinforced by Low's argumentative and
didactic bent. The problem came back to mass democracy again:
people needed to be made to think, and the potent weapons of
ridicule and satire were the best way for the cartoonist to stir them.

When Frank Swinnerton commented on Low's 'pep', he went
on to draw an immediate contrast with the 'good breeding' that
traditionally dominated British cartoons. Low was a breath of
fresh air in this sense too. Only Will Dyson, also schooled on
the *Bulletin*, had cast off Victorian gentility with much success
already, and he had done so on the small-circulation Labour *Daily
Herald* for a few years chiefly before the First World War.

Low reacted against a convention of humour typified in the
late Victorian *Punch*, in which cartoons, in Max Beerbohm's
phrase, were 'comic ideas, seriously illustrated'. Victorian values
made cartooning bland, 'not so much satirical commentating,'
Low argued, 'as humorous reporting'. Low repeatedly cited Tenniel as epitomising the application of artistic skill to innocuous
ends. 'Dropping the Pilot' 'passed all the tests of the upper-class
British ideal with such honours that it won everlasting fame of
the kind accorded to such works as "The Stag at Bay"'; while
its drawing was marked by a 'lack of "overloading" and a total
absence of humour, a stiffness of construction and a hardness of
technique'. Low thought Tenniel was a positive calamity for
satirical criticism.[41]

Low poked fun too at the 'superior preachy dignity' of John
Bull, and the sort of cartoon in which Bull congratulates some
proconsul with the words 'Well done, Sir! England is proud of

you!' (He put the words in Neville Chamberlain's mouth in a Topical Budget.) He criticised Ruskin for applauding the lack of any *'degeneration'* into caricature in the humour of Du Maurier, Leech and their contemporaries. 'Caricatures had ceased to be a lark and had become a solemn old owl.'[42]

Low's heroes, as already mentioned, were Gillray and Rowlandson. He identified himself sufficiently with Gillray to write and broadcast an imaginary dialogue between Gillray and himself (not without, it might be said, a touch of the John Bulls itself: 'With you, Sir, caricature ceased to be an aberration of artists and became itself an art'). Of the continentals, Philipon and Daumier received unqualified praise. Philipon's magazine *La Caricature* was 'a peak point in the history of satirical art in all countries'.[43] Daumier's drawing of the murdered family in 'Rue Transnonain' was 'the dramatic chef d'oeuvre of satire'. ('That,' wrote Low in a characteristic observation, 'is a sad leg.') His admiration for Max Beerbohm has been described; and although their political attitudes were utterly different (and are nicely compared in John Rothenstein's introduction to the King Penguin edition of Beerbohm's *The Poet's Corner*) Beerbohm shared Low's view of the limitations of Victorian graphic humour. Even though he could not 'draw' in the conventional sense, Beerbohm told Low, he would infinitely rather be himself than, say, Bernard Partridge: 'It must be awful to be a slave to skill in exactly literal representation of men and things. But to have all the elements of that skill and to override them and have them merely as a starting-point seems to me a very fortunate and enviable condition.' Such, he indicated, was Low's situation, 'And I would, therefore, infinitely rather be Low than Max.'[44]

Low thus saw himself, as did his audience at the time, breaking new ground in the newspaper cartoon, and returning to the spirit of the late eighteenth and early nineteenth centuries – before the 'Glacial Period or Nice Age'. The only drawback about the modern newspaper was that while Gillray sold prints over the shop counter, the newspaper reader bought the cartoon as part of a package and in such numbers that editors were bound to emphasise entertainment, simplicity and inoffensiveness at the expense of subtlety and controversy. The bite became a graze.

Even a graze, however, was better than the wet nuzzle of Low's predecessors. Low gave due credit to the *Bulletin* for developing the right spirit in him. 'The Sydney *Bulletin* under the editorship of Jack Archibald and James Edmond and the proprietorship of William Macleod was, I think, second only to the school of

Philipon, the ideal school for caricatures. A living policy in the making of a continent, plenty of space, no restrictions, and damn the consequences. I thank God I served my apprenticeship in such a school.'[45]

But Low talked tougher than he persistently seemed. The quotation from Paul Nash at the beginning of this chapter is typical. Some of his *Bulletin* colleagues, such as C. R. Bradish, felt he went a bit soft in London: 'his lampoonery soon acquired the air of Piccadilly; after six months of London it was wearing a club necktie'. But on the *Bulletin* too he had not seemed unduly cruel. He could criticise without a sneer, as Bradish put it.[46] If the Victorians wanted comic ideas seriously illustrated, Low gave their successors serious ideas comically illustrated. Low could not help clothing even the brute stupidity of Blimp in an amiable shape.

As he always said, Low liked people. He did not mean his cartoons personally and seems to have been surprised if people took them so. As he passed the Law Courts with a friend one day, he was greeted from the opposite pavement by Joynson-Hicks ('Jix') – as already mentioned, a favourite butt. Low waved back. 'I always salute my material,' he told his friend.[47] Though trivial, it is a revealing anecdote; not least, without giving it too much weight, for the use of the respectful 'salute', rather than the weaker 'acknowledge'. When Oswald Mosley discovered he was at a dinner party where Low and Lloyd George would meet, he expected fireworks: 'This is going to be good.' In fact, of course, Low and Lloyd George got on well.[48]

Low's good nature flowed out through his brush. But can he have 'liked' Hitler and Mussolini? Certainly he felt the best way for a cartoonist to contribute to their downfall was by ridicule, as was seen in the previous chapter. Sheer hate was less effective, in or out of wartime. Low claimed to care little how his cartoons affected their subjects' happiness. But the artist's own goals were better achieved by humour. In *Ye Madde Designer*, written before the dictators' zenith, he wrote that 'no artist in caricature purely can do good work on malice. It clouds the judgement. The immoderate exaggeration inspired by malice is apt to become as tedious as too much slapstick in a farce . . . Brutality almost invariably defeats itself.'[49] In peacetime it was no doubt easy to make such assertions. Still in 1937 Anthony Blunt could take the same side, arguing that it was Low's very kindness that made his cartoons savage. If they sprang from hate, their victims could more easily dismiss them: 'It is the condemnation of the just man that strikes home so acutely.'[50]

A movement is reported in Moscow against the children's conventional toys, especially dolls, which are held to be non-Communist, reactionary and injurious. Low fears the worst may happen to those which, when pressed in the Tumski, utter the bourgeois words "Ma-ma-Pa-pa".

SHOT AT DAWN

THE RUSSIAN TERROR AGAIN.

The consistency of Low's view, as far even as the treatment of the dictators in wartime, no doubt reflected his conviction that styles of cartoon varied with national temperament. His geniality made an obvious contrast with the bitter, cruel, sometimes hate-filled work of continental cartoonists represented in such French periodicals as *Le Rire*, *L'Assiette au Beurre*, *Le Charivari* and their successors, and in their German counterparts such as *Kladderadatsch* and *Simplicissimus*. But bitterness and mordancy 'won't do – in this country. It defeats its own ends. Your cartoon must have urbanity, fairness, humour.' Again, 'the history of art in England shows us that it is easier to impress an Englishman by exciting his sense of humour than by exciting his sense of horror'. More is the pity, he added, since '"hate" ideas full of blood and bones, and drawn with plenty of ink, would be much easier to produce'.[51] In specialised magazines, moreover, it might be possible to publish work quite unacceptable to a mass-circulation daily paper.

145 'The Russian terror again', *Evening Standard*, 22 April 1930

When conventional toys were attacked in the Moscow press as 'non-communistic, reactionary and injurious' Low set up this new 'terror' tribunal, with Stalin, Litvinoff and Rykoff in charge. Low nearly always preferred to score points through mockery, even on a subject with grim undertones.

Low's geniality, then, is rooted firmly in the same culture as the Victorian gentility which he scorned. He broke down some of its constraints, which were foreign to his antipodean background. But he remained within an utterly English tradition. The point can perhaps be made best by contrasting him, say, with George Grosz, a homegrown critic of rottenness in interwar Germany. Grosz's Expressionist criticism is blood and bones, war or no war. Low, on the other hand, is a bourgeois realist through and through, with a style that perfectly matched his feeling for his popular audience. In his art, as in his relation to London life and politics – and to his employer – Low established himself as an original voice of self-confidence and individuality, but tight within the clutch of the popular values of his time.

III Low's Attitudes

Time and again Low would throw a couple of bones for inter-viewers to gnaw. 'If you're ever asked to write my epitaph you can say: Here lies a nuisance who was dedicated to sanity.' That was one. 'To me,' went the other, 'there has always seemed to be more stupidity than wickedness in the world.'[1]

Style and substance interweave. As Low's style matured early, so did his political beliefs. One observer noted during Low's eighth British general election, in 1950, that his message was much the same as at the first, in 1922.[2] At that one too his views had reflected attitudes already settled in New Zealand and Australia. Some of them will be clear from the previous chapters. For specific events and issues, the cartoons in this book provide illustrations. This chapter simply aims to trace enduring themes in Low's beliefs and to indicate in particular the nature of his professed radicalism.

'Sanity' and 'stupidity', often contrasted, were key concepts. The latter, by its contrast also with wickedness, implies a benign view of human nature. If only man were not so stupid, he would make less mess of the world. (Blimp, transparently, is stupid not wicked.) While Low was thus a firm believer in the fallibility of man, he was at the same time an optimist. 'The spectacle of Devon living at peace with Somerset fills me with hope for the future,' he wrote in 1934. '"This is marvellous," I say to myself; "... all these animals have learned to live together sensibly in peace, without flying at each other's throats."' He believed in progress; in education as a force for good; in the improbability (in 1956) that he would ever have to draw an atomic war.[3]

Progress involves applying the dictates of reason: 'Even as a youngster I distrusted the emotional approach to politics. To my mind an ounce of calm deliberation was worth a ton of indignation ...'[4] A rational world would mean overcoming ignorance and abandoning stupidities inherited from the past – or not seeking to recreate them, as he felt English Conservatives wanted after the First World War. Low's radicalism started as a rational, youthful idealism. It was tempered over the years to a pragmatic reformism, so that by the time postwar reconstruction was on the agenda in 1944, when he was in his early fifties, he could tell the *Chicago*

"I KNOW WHAT IT NEEDS, BOSS! FOUNDATIONS!"

146 'I know what it needs, boss! Foundations!', *Evening Standard*, 19 July 1943

R. A. Butler's White Paper on education was published in 1943. Low approved of the Paper's aim to establish a tripartite secondary system up to the age of fifteen. He puts Butler's 'education cement' to good use producing mortar to reinforce the institution of democracy.

Sun: 'I am sick of all this obsolete rot about "class war". The only class war I am interested in is that between the sane and insane.'[5]

Above all, as we have seen, Low was at heart an individualist; and the independence of mind and action that he wished for himself, he wished also for others. This meant not only a lack of deference in manner ('God Save the King!' 'Why,' asks the child Low, 'what's *he* done?') but also a belief that people should work things out for themselves. When conscription was invoked in New Zealand as a domestic defence measure, before the First World War was even on the horizon, the adolescent Low, typically, was all against it.[6]

154

One of Low's first published cartoons, back in the piano-case days, was about sanity (a lunatic asylum). The essence of sanity, in Low's usage, is balance. With balance, style and substance most plainly interweave. Even Low's signature is a carefully drawn symmetrical arrangement of the letters of his surname that conveys an effect of balance. A balanced view of how to behave as an individual, and how the world should behave as a whole, implies the possession of a sense of proportion, the denial of extremism and the shunning of zealotry. Yet, as Low pointed out, a sense of proportion is effectively the same as a sense of humour. 'Taking things to extremes' – of argument or behaviour, as of physical proportions – is the cartoonist's method of demonstrating absurdity. By his ignorance or insensitiveness to alternatives, a cartoon character is made ridiculous, unaware of that contrast between 'what is and what could be' that Low regarded as defining a sense of the ridiculous. Insane people (at least in the lay use of the term) are ridiculous – unbalanced – in exactly this way. They are oblivious of alternative ways of looking at things, and more especially of the way regarded popularly as sane (which sometimes, of course, is disputed). Part of Blimp's absurdity is his utter ('insane') conviction that his outbursts make sense.

In the political sphere the denial of alternative ways of looking at things is an assertion of infallibility. Extremism and zealotry stifle individualism and license oppression. Extreme devotion to leaders flatters and blinkers them and tickles them into corruption. Low inherited the traditional liberal view that the only correct view of society is the view which maintains that there is no correct view. You may prefer one course of action over another, but you must win other people to it by reason, not by force or assertion. Low's antipathy to Fascism (including Mosley's) and eventually to Stalinist Russia, was the classic liberal opposition to unreason and intolerance. Leaders of all kinds needed constant reducing to appropriate proportions by the touch of the satirist. In a farewell article in the *Bulletin* in 1919 Low criticised Australian governments for 'arrogating to themselves too much power' and regarding the people as 'herds of unruly cattle to be driven hither and thither as Governmental audacity might dictate'.[7] In his early years on the *Star* he showed politicians pursuing inconsistent or foolish goals; motivated by selfishness over such problems as the coal industry and German reparations; failing to learn the lessons of the war or of Irish policy; failing to deliver jobs and 'homes fit for heroes'; and quick to claim credit when any was going. He labelled them 'Misrepresentatives'. In the mid-1930s he was

147 'Grand 5th November fireworks display', *Star, c.* 1926

After the General Strike in May 1926 there was not a complete return to work in the coal industry until December.

This cartoon criticises Baldwin, the Prime Minister (wearing a mask of Evan Williams, spokesman of the mine owners), for dilatoriness in using opportunities, such as the Samuel Report of the previous March, to bring peace to the industry.

GRAND 5TH NOVEMBER FIREWORKS DISPLAY

doing much the same thing, but with a greater emphasis on international politics. In 1950, he responded to criticisms of 'disloyalty' to his new employer, the *Daily Herald*, with a ponderous cartoon in which he drew himself calling to a barmaid, 'Fill 'em up again, Miss! The toast is Merrie Socialist Britain where we can still treat our leaders as human beings, not gods, and keep our ideals fresh and healthy by giving them a good bath of satire every weekend.'[8]

Such a view of 'sanity' buttressed Low's refusal to commit himself unreservedly to any political creed or party. He was disinclined by temperament anyway to carry unnecessary intellectual baggage. He had the auto-didact's suspicion of the overly intellectual. 'I was always more impressed by intelligence than by intellect,' he remarked near the end of his life.[9] As to parties, they were human institutions subject to human failings. It is unclear how far Low was a 'party activist' (to use a latter-day term) in New Zealand and Australia, and, if so, for how long. But the choice in London must have been simple for a man with such

A CARTOON FOR A DISSATISFIED CUSTOMER

a streak of independence and a strong personality. He might, like Will Dyson, have become a fierce Labour loyalist, but it was much more in character for him to stay detached. The natural condition of the cartoonist, after all, is opposition. He summed up his viewpoint when he left the *Star*: 'I am a Radical. But no party can lay exclusive claims to virtue. My political cartoons in the "Standard" will be non-party, and as such they will, I feel, afford me a wider scope.'[10] Part of the attraction of Gillray was that Gillray had not been a good party man, as Low says in their broadcast 'dialogue':

LOW: Since stupidity is no monopoly of any one party, no conscientious caricaturist can be a party man. Let those that can think follow ideas; those that can't must follow leaders. I am

148 'A cartoon for a dissatisfied customer', *Daily Herald*, 25 April 1950

Idealised versions of Cripps, Attlee, Morrison and the Common Man (and Low!) are contrasted with their workaday selves (including the "World Citizen"). Just because he was now working for a paper controlled by the Labour Movement, Low was not going to treat Labour leaders as anything other than humanly fallible.

not puzzled, therefore, as some are, by the fact that on occasion you worked against both parties.

GILLRAY: When they were both ridiculous.[11]

Even in the Second World War Low did not simplify the issues to unqualified Good versus Evil. Hitler himself seemed almost more stupid than wicked – a simple man uncomplicated by pity. What we were fighting for, Low told listeners to the BBC Pacific Service in 1944, was not 'the soil' or 'a new world', but for 'a good number of different ways of life . . ., all, including our own, leaving a good deal to be desired'. The virtue of our own was its basis in reason, unlike the insane emotionalism of the dictators.[12]

Low's professional non-partisanship did not deter him from contributing privately to Labour Party funds.[13] But one wonders whether even this commitment survived the war, for his opinions on the party system became increasingly caustic. Already in 1941 he was saying, 'Sometimes it seems that the correct party designations of the future world should be the Intelligent Party versus the Stupid Party.' When he joined the *Daily Herald* he told an interviewer, 'there's a lot of hooey talked about parties. A good man's a good man and a bone-headed idiot's a bone-headed idiot, whatever party he belongs to.'[14] Life at the *Herald* confirmed his opinion. In the mid-1950s Low shared the common view that the parties now differed chiefly in the pace at which they managed change: a 'Hurry Up' party and a 'Go Slow' party would reflect realities. A clear-cut Opposition, he became fond of saying, would come only from a party of Order confronting a party of Freedom, 'the one placing the emphasis on planning, regulation and duty, and the other on the enlargement of the sphere of individual liberty'.[15]

The product of Low's view of human nature and institutions, his guiding principles – and his personal ambitions – was a moderate radicalism. In method it was pragmatic, Fabian, reformist. His reservations about political leaders and parties did not qualify his commitment, even as a young man, to the idea of parliamentary government. His optimism and belief in the potential of reason made him a convinced constitutionalist. For him the lesson of the General Strike in 1926, for instance, was that the Labour movement should work through the existing political framework: 'It is less trouble to go through the door than to push the walls down. Revolutionary strikes don't mix with political democracy.' Later he fell out with the Jews on similar grounds, for he disapproved

158

149 'The flight that failed', *Star*, *c.* 1926

Low's comment on the failure of the General Strike reflected his deep-rooted commitment to constitutional methods of achieving social and economic change.

THE FLIGHT THAT FAILED
Or, the hardest way up is the easiest way there

of the violent means by which the state of Israel was established.[16]

Low was the sort of person who likes to say that parliamentary democracy is the 'least worst' form of government. He explained it to an American audience as an example of that 'peculiar kind of untidiness which is Britain's most valuable contribution to civilisation'.[17] Twenty-five years earlier he had not minded the 'untidiness' which saw Labour leaders such as MacDonald and Thomas consorting with duchesses and wearing upper-class clothes. Perhaps because of his background, Low's was a very un-class-conscious radicalism. The fundamental freedom, regardless of class, was that people should have the chance to express themselves freely. Part of the untidiness of democracy was that not enough people took advantage of it. Low had criticised Australians for their narrow vision, and he criticised the British for it too.[18]

The Second World War saw a culmination of these views. Low was dismayed at the level of popular ignorance about the roots of the war and at its justification by an appeal to primitive passions. Hence the publication of *Europe since Versailles*.[19] A few years later, he gave vent to his feelings in an unpublished open letter to a serviceman, 'Walter', who wrote expressing disillusion with the prospects of postwar Britain. Come back, urged Low. Thoughtful people were all too few. 'Only a minute proportion of our people, I suppose, takes a rational interest in politics, trying to view the whole picture, to estimate possibilities and to count consequences. The remaining crowd includes those who don't look beyond their own noses, those who can't see straight for passion and those who are too busy with love and sport to spare a glance at their own destinies. Naturally, when it comes to politics, this crowd tends to bank, not on cool judgement of ideas, but on personalities, party labels, catch-cries and headlines. Naturally, also, politics push them around, they fall over themselves, they find themselves continually chased up alleys with nothing to show for all their cheers and boos but a kick on the pants. They ask for it, and they get it. No political system could do more for them. None ever has. Blame not the political system. We have a political system better than most. It has proved its soundness in war. It is adequate to build a healthy nation in peace, too – but only if it be tended sensibly. My generation hasn't done too well with it. It's going to be up to you and your generation of fighting youth to do better, Walter.'[20]

After the war, Low became much more consciously didactic. By 1950 he was describing himself as a Social Democrat, plainly more concerned with how things should be done than with what to do – which he considered, at least in domestic policy, to be largely common ground.

Low started out, then, as a reformist committed to parliamentary democracy. The experience of Europe in the 1930s, of the Second World War and of the Cold War, entrenched his beliefs while making him urgently aware of the fragility of parliamentary institutions in the absence of active popular support. His own potential role as a popular educator was a preoccupation of the postwar years and found an outlet in such ideas as the World Citizen strip.

If the method of political progress became virtually more important to Low than its substance, that substance remained firmly progressive. It may fairly be described, in its British context, as 'Left-Liberal' – hardly systematic enough, certainly on

"DAMMIT, YOUNG MAN, WE MUSTN'T PUT THE CART BEFORE THE HORSE!"

150 'Dammit, young man, we mustn't put the cart before the horse!', *Evening Standard*, 26 June 1944

Low supported the kind of social planning envisaged in documents such as the Beveridge Report. His cartoons at this time label 'private interests' as reactionary and anti-social. 'I had a door to the masses which they had not, but it soon became evident that many people, if they did not positively deplore my giving a wider currency to such matters as socially unsettling, thought that the medium of caricature was unseemly as a means.' (*Autobiography*, p. 351)

the evidence of his cartoons, to be called socialist. The *Economist*, reviewing *Years of Wrath* in 1949, accurately described Low as 'the favourite cartoonist of the Left-Centre intelligentsia of England – indeed of the English-speaking world.'[21]

Low's individualism and his Australasian background gave his views a strong flavour of egalitarianism. Australians talk of the 'tall poppy' syndrome, the national habit of cutting down stems that outstrip their fellows. Low had a predictable distaste for the snobberies and inequalities of British society and experienced them at first hand. To his friend Kingsley Martin, he retained something of a colonial chip on his shoulder. His alignment of himself in his cartoons with the ordinary man was more than a stylistic device. 'His inclination runs to the democratic taste for taking people down a peg,' commented V. S. Pritchett.[22] His opinion of the low political sophistication of the mass electorate reflected not a patronising contempt but a belief that it stemmed from ignorance and could be dispelled by education.

Beyond this general fellow-feeling, however, Low was chiefly concerned with equality of opportunity. He was a tall poppy himself, and while there is no reason to suppose his ambitions would have been 'cut down' if he had stayed in Australia, we have seen how some of his colleagues felt he was ruthlessly concerned for success.

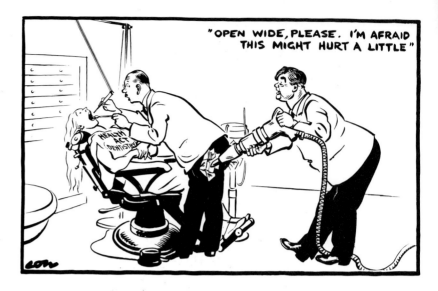

151 'Open wide, please. I'm afraid this might hurt a little', *Evening Standard*, 9 December 1948

Many doctors and dentists took a great deal of persuading that Aneurin Bevan's National Health Service would not harm the interests of the medical profession – and indirectly, therefore, of patients.

Inequality of rewards did not worry Low much. 'Lords, after all, are not always lords for nothing.'[23] He believed in the virtue of hard work. Wealth and success, in any case, were not the keys to happiness. Happiness, as he argued at some length in his contribution to a book of *Sermons by Artists* in 1934, was to be found rather in simplicity ('the simplicity of sanity') and love ('the spirit of goodwill').

In preferring the sort of equality that would give men and women the chance to fulfil their individual potential, Low joined, so to speak, the 'Freedom Party'. But what about the 'Order Party'? 'In any ideal world,' Low told the Ruskin Society in 1935, 'the necessities of life, easily produced, are easily got, freeing man from this everlasting preoccupation with continuing existence. I do not mind being an Economic Machine-man for an hour or two per day, if I am free for the rest of the day to develop my individuality to engage in the Higher Private Enterprise, to civilise myself.' To H. G. Wells Low argued, similarly, 'I have use for socialism only so far as it helps us all to grow to our full stature mentally as well as physically.'[24]

Low accepted readily the need for curbs on individuality for the sake of the common good. His farewell to the *Bulletin* stressed that 'real progress lies in political and economic altruism'. In 1941 he looked forward hopefully to the postwar foundation of 'the collective principles by which only we may secure our well-being' while at the same time enhancing individual prospects.[25] The Labour Government's welfare legislation was exactly the kind of programme he approved.

The state, in sum, was for Low a framework within which

LET US CONSIDER

MAN,

THE LORD OF CREATION.

152 *Man, the Lord of Creation,* London, Putman, 1920

In the two-dozen little drawings published as *Man* (1920) Low mocked man's selfish and destructive materialism. It was 'an admirable jest and an admirable piece of morality', commented the reviewer Robert Lynd. 'Anyone who knows a hard-faced man should send it to him as a Christmas card.'

economic and social well-being could be guaranteed and political freedoms maintained. Good government, plainly, is 'sane': it relieves 'stupidity'. In developing this outlook Low said he was much influenced as a youth by the utopian novel *Looking Backward, 2000–1887*, published by the American Edward Bellamy in 1888. He named it as one of the three most influential books he ever read. (For the rest, he could not choose between Tolstoy, Shaw and Wells.) Bellamy's vision incorporates the kind of combination of communal organisation and individual scope (more in the economic and social than the political sphere) that, in principle, appealed to Low. Low's outlook is encapsulated, too, in his little book *Man, the Lord of Creation*, published in 1920. This is a fable, with very little text – very much a publishing curiosity. Its theme is the destructive effect of man's selfish material ambitions upon his environment, his fellow-creatures and his own potential. 'Man' is drawn foolish rather than wicked. His actions are the folly, too, of the 'insane': 'owing to the cost of putting a barb-wire fence around this food, fellow-creatures will in future be charged a small fee for corn'.

Low applied the same ideas, of course, to international affairs.

153 'Progress to liberty – Amritsar style', *Star*, *c.* April 1919

The massacre of Indian civilians at Amritsar by British troops on 13 April 1919 roused passions both among supporters and opponents of Indian nationalism. Low recalled: 'There was a row. This was a cartoon so far removed from the customary pleasantries that it shocked. For some days sizzling letters poured in . . .' (*Autobiography*, p. 98). The cartoon is a good example of Low's use of contrasting masses of black and white in his designs.

PROGRESS TO LIBERTY – AMRITSAR STYLE

He had a natural antipathy to colonialism, bitterly expressed in 'Progress to liberty – Amritsar style' (1919). Diehard imperialism, such as Churchill's towards India in the 1930s, was a fruitful source of blimpishness ('There must be no monkeying with the liberty of Indians to do what they're dashed well told'). His background enabled him to identify instinctively with the movement of Empire into Commonwealth, and to appreciate the significance of the Pacific theatre and the reorientation of Australia towards the USA in the Second World War. Like liberals in general, he saw that the war was changing the Empire irreversibly. 'The battle-cries of freedom and independence ultimately belong to the brown and black skins too as much as to those who happen to be white.'[26]

He had a similar sympathy with the USA and described himself as by nature a sort of honorary American. 'I had had to learn

154 *New York Times Magazine*, 20 July 1952

The picture accompanied an article Low wrote for the *New York Times*, headed 'Cartoonist Low sketches the half-truths that cloud the picture of Anglo–US understanding.'

the English but I felt I knew most about Americans to start with.'[27] 'The land of opportunity' and of other homespun values might have been expected to appeal to him more strongly than class-conscious Britain. But in fact he found less scope for individualism and too much esteem for material success. Franklin Roosevelt, of course, was his sort of man, and the New Deal was an obvious expression of 'sanity'. Low clearly enjoyed mediating the British and Americans to each other in his articles and broadcasts in the 1940s and early 1950s.

Low reacted instinctively against Japanese militarism and expansion into Chinese Manchuria, just as he predictably supported the Republicans in Spain and belittled Franco as a jesterlike figure. The USSR was more complex. The turning point was 'Rendezvous', Low's cartoon marking the Nazi–Soviet pact in 1939, when the 'assassin of the workers' and 'the scum of the earth' cynically allied in the ruins of Poland. Throughout the interwar period Low had been ready to show a matter-of-fact goodwill to the Soviets, and he became quite a close friend of the Soviet ambassador Maisky. With the rise of Fascism in the 1930s, he thought it was commonsense not to alienate Stalin: the pact was simply the end of a period of increasingly foolish exclusion and it left the European democracies isolated before Hitler. After the war, Low's sympathy dwindled. He was still willing to look at things from Russia's point of view, but, as Kingsley Martin suggested in 1956, 'like the rest of us, he has had to admit that totalitarianism in Moscow has turned out as bad as anywhere else'.[28]

"WHO'S NEXT TO BE LIBERATED FROM FREEDOM, COMRADE?"

155 'Who's next to be liberated from freedom, comrade?', *Evening Standard*, 2 March 1948

Low expresses a conventional Cold War suspicion of Stalin's ambitions. His interwar sympathy with the Soviet regime, certainly in foreign affairs, is a thing of the past.

If Devon and Somerset had learnt to live together, why not the rest of the world? Low was ever an internationalist, so his cartoons consistently looked to the potential of the League of Nations and the United Nations. First he favoured disarmament and collective security under the League. When Mussolini successfully defied the League in annexing Abyssinia, Low was for backing the League with force. When Hitler occupied the Rhineland in 1936 and stepped up his aggression, Low called for faster rearmament. With the Czech crisis in 1938, Low 'rampaged'.[29] Those changes coincided directly with the policy neither of the Government, locked into appeasement and suspicious of Russia, nor of the Conservative Right, nor of the several strands of opinion in the Labour movement. Low was not an isolated voice, of course; but his pragmatic individualism could not be better illustrated. Here indeed was a nuisance dedicated to sanity, vindicated in the stupidity of a second world war.

166

IV Low's Impact

Low gave a good fifty years of amusement and instruction. He found words and images to sum up what an audience rippling into worldwide millions felt about their times. They wrote to tell him – to say how much they agreed or (more often) disagreed with him and to call him a Bloody New Zealand Gorilla or a Jew ('Mr Löwe'). They pointed out mistakes. Moors do not have negroid faces, nor do runners have spikes in the heels of their shoes. The Swastika should go the other way round, Union Jacks (Gad, Sir!) the other way up and circular saws should revolve in the other direction. Cartwheels should have an even number of spokes, otherwise they buckle ('You have been guilty on previous occasions'). 'For heaven's sake when you try and draw an elephant again do go to the Zoo . . .' 'The idea of the lookout deckhouse abaft the funnel is absurd . . .' They wrote to ask if they might name their racehorse after him and bring parties to visit his studio. They sent him amended copies of his cartoons and ideas of their own. They sought advice on cartooning as a career.

All this reflects impact of a kind. But did Low strike deeper? Stalin was said to have a Low original on his office wall, at least when Churchill visited Moscow in 1942. What did it do to him when he looked at it? How far did Low influence attitudes among his audience of millions, as well as reflecting them?

His contemporaries certainly believed Low's influence over popular attitudes was great. Obviously Low himself would have liked it to be so. From around the mid-1930s, as we have seen, he aspired increasingly to an educational role. Beaverbrook claimed that the *Evening Standard* circulation rose by 50,000 after Low joined it. This was an extravagant claim: it would have been a rise of some fifteen per cent and unlikely to be entirely attributable to Low. Besides, the paper's circulation went down as well as up during the 1930s, and, at 382,000 in 1939, it was still 40,000 below the figure at which Beaverbrook took it over in 1923. The evidence of opinion surveys since the 1940s suggests that it is usually very difficult for news media to influence opinions in specific, intended directions. Low is more likely, on this evidence, to have influenced what people thought *about* than what they actually

JUST IN CASE THERE'S ANY MISTAKE

Low's popular impact is difficult to estimate. How far in a cartoon such as this was he reflecting popular opinion, and how far forming it? His own determination, in either case, is clear. There must be no vacillation by Chamberlain and Halifax.

thought, and to have reinforced their opinions rather than changed them. But the readiness of politicians to believe that Low influenced people was an influence in itself, for the belief might change the politicians' own behaviour.

The clearest examples of politicians affected by Low are the attempts at censorship discussed in Chapter I, both at home (including, by extension, the official treatment of the Blimp film) and by Hitler, Mussolini and Franco. But such behaviour was directed at Low himself. There is no evidence whether politicians behaved differently towards anyone else as a result of Low's cartoons. The former Downing Street official Tom Jones told Low he had 'forced' Baldwin, when Prime Minister, to look at some Low clippings, but there is no reason to suppose they changed Baldwin's mind about anything.[1] Of course, politicians generally enjoyed being in cartoons as a mark of distinction, and some of them may indeed have adapted their public performances to fit Low's cartoon props. But that is a matter of externals.

Beaverbrook's predecessor Lord Northcliffe, founder of the *Daily Mail* and most colossal of press barons, said: 'The whole world will think with us when we say the word.' That was a delusion. No more should one think that Low could quake the

ON TOUR

earth with a cartoon. Attitudes are formed, rather, by a slither of shifting forces. On the other hand, surely Low was one such force. The lack of hard evidence should not be pushed too far. 'When the history of these odd times comes to be written,' the historian Bernard Pares wrote to Low in 1941, his cartoons would be 'the best pointer of all.' Harold Laski wrote similarly in 1945: 'I have thought your cartoons this month or so about the best social history anyone is writing today.'[2]

Low had a sense of the way that history was moving. It is as though he rose from his thinking ditch in New Zealand and followed a star. '*MADE GOOD* – Dave Low Goes to England.' The newspaper headline was an honest recognition that a great

157 'On tour', *Evening Standard*, 30 June 1945

Churchill harangues voters on the evils of nationalisation and social planning in the run-up to the first postwar general election. But Low proved a better judge of the mood of the British voter. (Labour was returned with an overall majority of 146.) The 'Dead Duck' inn sign adds a nice Hogarthian touch.

talent is nourished by great events. Low provoked strong reaction in huge audiences so frequently, and he was so palpably in touch with them in a symbiotic way, that talk of impact in the abrupt manner of an earthquake is too crude. Low's influence, surely, was more atmospheric, part of the air people breathed.

Low was rarely compared to a Court Jester but the image would fit. A Jester was close to his King and could speak the truth, masked by jest, that other men dared not speak. Low, like the Jester, was a man somewhat apart, with a detachment half professional and half due to his background. The Jester, though damned for a fool, might be the sanest man at court, like the little boy who saw that the Emperor had no clothes. Low kept company (literally to some extent) with the leaders of his time – the 'Kings'. He drew the truth as he saw it, with unrivalled success in getting through to a mass audience. He was the supreme newspaper cartoonist of his times and for his times; and in being so, he fulfilled himself.

158 'The End', *A Cartoon History of Our Times*, New York, Simon & Schuster, 1939

Low's tailpiece for his American anthology, *A Cartoon History of Our Times*. Note Neville Chamberlain's moustache and teeth next to the top hat.

References

Unpublished sources are in the Low Papers except where otherwise stated.

CHAPTER I

1. *Low's Autobiography*, London, Michael Joseph, 1956, p. 27. (Henceforth abbreviated as *LA*.)
2. *LA*, p. 47.
3. *Ibid.*, p. 43.
4. *Ibid.*, p. 57.
5. George Robertson to Low, 28 June 1920, Angus & Robertson Papers, Mitchell Library, Sydney, NSW.
6. *LA*, p. 70.
7. *Ibid.*
8. Quoted by Patricia Rolfe in *Journalistic Javelin*, Sydney, Wildcat Press, 1979, pp. 263–4.
9. *LA*, p. 251
10. *Bulletin*, 21(?) November 1921.
11. Low Papers, Box 11.
12. *LA*, p. 125.
13. This was a story Low told often. See e.g. *Strand Magazine*, September 1926.
14. Stuart Hodgson, *New Era*, 1 July 1929.
15. *LA*, p. 102.
16. *Ibid.*, p. 130.
17. Kipling to Low, 2 September 1926.
18. Garvin to Sharp, 2 February 1926.
19. Wells to Low, 26 January 1926; Beaverbrook to Low, 26 September 1928.
20. William Mellor to Low, 23 September 1926.
21. *Star* contract dated 25 September 1924, Beaverbrook Papers, House of Lords Record Office.
22. *LA*, p. 182.
23. *The Press*, Christchurch, 23 December 1949; *LA*, p. 182.
24. Sharp to Low, 17 November 1927.
25. *LA*, p. 183.
26. *Ibid.*, p. 182.
27. *Report on the British Press*, London, PEP, 1938, p. 235.
28. Beaverbrook to Low, 20 June 1938.
29. A. J. P. Taylor, *Beaverbrook*, London, Hamish Hamilton, 1972, p. 216.
30. Beaverbrook to Low, 10 May 1934.
31. *Daily Express*, 5 December 1957.
32. *Star* contract, 25 September 1924, Beaverbrook Papers.
33. Correspondence of Low and Michael Wardell, January 1934.
34. Halifax to Beaverbrook, 6 May 1940, Public Record Office file FO 371/34500.
35. *LA*, p. 197.
36. Percy Cudlipp to Low, 24 November 1936.
37. Tiquet to Low, 30 July 1936.
38. *The Windsorian*, April 1935.
39. 'Wisdom Book: David Low with Percy Cudlipp', NBC-TV, 1960. Transcript in Low Papers.
40. *LA*, p. 284.
41. Low to Thompson, 24 July 1938.
42. *Time*, 29 December 1947.
43. *Sunday Graphic*, 28 November 1938; Kingsley Martin to Low, 24 November 1938.
44. Marjorie Spence to Low, 2 September 1933.
45. Wells to Low, 25 August 1929; *LA*, p. 284.
46. *Listener*, 14 December 1932; *Manchester Guardian*, 10 December 1932.
47. Kingsley Martin, *Editor*, London, Hutchinson, 1968, p. 62.
48. *Observer*, 12 July 1942.
49. *LA*, pp. 285, 303.
50. Low to Guedalla, 28 July 1928; Guedalla to Low, 28 July 1928; *LA*, p. 141.
51. Beaverbrook to Low, 3 December 1934.
52. *LA*, p. 289.
53. Rebecca West to Low, 28 December 1934.
54. William Rothenstein to Low, (?) March 1942.
55. Low to Rosenwald, 11 April 1941.
56. *New Statesman*, 5 January 1942, 9 August 1941.
57. Beaverbrook to Low, 27 July 1928.

58. Humphrey Jennings to Low, 10 January 1936.
59. For an account of this episode, see Ian Christie (ed.), *Powell, Pressburger and Others*, London, British Film Institute, 1978.
60. *Evening Standard*, 20 July 1928.
61. *Listener*, 15 February 1940; *LA*, p. 336.
62. *Evening Standard*, 2 July 1936.
63. *LA*, p. 218.
64. *Punch*, 7 May 1930.
65. *New York World Telegram*, 26 October 1936.
66. *The Times*, 12 May 1937.
67. *LA*, p. 212.
68. E.g. *Manchester Guardian*, 1 November 1938; *The Times*, 19 August 1936.
69. Michael Wardell to Low, 15 June 1936.
70. *LA*, p. 279.
71. *The Times*, 20 November 1936; *Listener*, 26 August 1936; *Time and Tide*, 9 September 1944; *Lilliput*, 12 August 1937.
72. *Spectator*, 6 March 1942; *New York Times Magazine*, 26 April 1942.
73. 'R.S.', *Star*, 3 July 1936.
74. *LA*, p. 333.
75. *Manchester Guardian*, 17 and 20 December 1945.
76. House of Commons, Official Report, 16 October 1939, col. 410.
77. *LA*, pp. 323, 347; Low to E. J. Robertson, 8 May 1942.
78. *LA*, p. 348.
79. Low Papers, Box 4.
80. Low to Kingsley Martin, 13 September 1956.
81. *The Times*, 22 November 1947; *Economist*, 9 July 1949. The Joss comment is in Low's cuttings book for July 1949 but without an attribution.
82. Herbert Gunn to Low, 19 March 1948; Low to Gunn, 22 March 1948.
83. *LA*, p. 373.
84. Beaverbrook to Low, 9 December 1949. Low mistranscribes the last sentence in his autobiography as 'Don't forget your old *friend*' (p. 379).
85. *Daily Herald*, 2 January 1950.
86. Christiansen to Low, 31 January 1950.
87. *Spectator*, 24 February 1950; *LA*, p. 381.
88. Interview with Colin Legum, *New Era*, 1952.
89. Low to Wadsworth, 1 July 1952; Wadsworth to Low, 1 July 1952; Low to Lawrence Scott, 1 August 1952; Low to Beaverbrook, 17 September 1929.
90. Low to Alastair Hetherington, 29 October 1959.
91. Wadsworth to Low, 28 March 1955.
92. Wadsworth to Low, 19 May 1953; Low to Wadsworth, 21 May 1953.
93. Wadsworth to Low, 3 and 5 June 1953.
94. Eliot to Low, 30 November 1945; Priestley to Low, 23 September 1945; Bevan to Low, 4 December 1945.
95. Waugh to Low, 19 November 1949.
96. *Observer*, 25 October 1953; *Times Literary Supplement*, 25 November 1960.
97. *Daily Telegraph*, Sydney (no doubt a syndicated review), 16 March 1957.
98. *New Era*, 1952.

CHAPTER II

1. *Bulletin*, 1 February 1933.
2. Jean Sibi, *Lone Hand*, 1 October 1915.
3. Beerbohm to Low, 18 February 1931; *Bookman*, New York, 1921; *Weekend Review*, 18 July 1931.
4. *World's Press News*, 23 January 1930; *Spectator*, 14 February 1931.
5. Ronald Searle, *Guardian*, 21 September 1963; Edmund Dulac, *Evening Standard*, 8 October 1927.
6. Quoted in *New Era*, 1952.
7. *LA*, p. 381.
8. *Spectator*, 14 May 1937.
9. *Ye Madde Designer*, pp. 10, 40; undated notes on caricature, Low Papers.
10. *Spectator*, 14 February 1931.
11. *Newspaper World*, 28 July 1949.
12. *News Chronicle*, 1944(?), Cuttings Book 13.
13. E. H. Gombrich, *Meditations on a Hobby Horse*, London, Phaidon Press, 1978, ch. 12.
14. *Newspaper World*, 28 July 1949.
15. *LA*, p. 94.
16. *Ibid.*, p. 381.
17. *Ibid.*, pp. 264–5.
18. *Evening Standard*, 14 October 1942.
19. *Ibid.*
20. E.g. Tom Driberg, *Leader Magazine*, 18 August 1945.
21. 'Adventures with My Pencil', *Strand Magazine*, September

1926; *British Cartoonists, Caricaturists and Comic Artists*, London, Collins, 1942, p. 10.

22. *Strand Magazine*, September 1926; *Nation and Athenaeum*, March (?) 1923.

23. H. L. Morrow in *Everyman*, 11 December 1930; *Listener*, 2 November 1939.

24. Ellen Wilkinson in *Now & Then*, Winter, 1930.

25. *Listener*, 26 August 1936.

26. Ellen Wilkinson, *op. cit.*

27. *Ibid.*

28. Encaenial Address, University of New Brunswick, undated; *Nation and Athenaeum*, 28 July 1928.

29. *Listener*, 8 December 1938.

30. Encaenial Address, University of New Brunswick, undated.

31. *Ye Madde Designer*, pp. 10–11, 36, 45, 52.

32. *Apollo*, December 1929.

33. *Spectator*, 14 February 1931; *The Poet's Corner*, London, Penguin Books, 1943, p. 6.

34. *Listener*, 1 March 1957.

35. *John O'London's Weekly*, 18 August 1928; *Evening Standard*, 26 January 1931; *Ye Madde Designer*, p. 67.

36. *Evening Standard*, 26 January 1931.

37. Letter to *The Press* (Christchurch, New Zealand), 3 December 1928.

38. *Observer*, 18 September 1927.

39. *Newspaper World*, 28 July 1949.

40. *Listener*, 2 December 1943; Foreword to H. R. Westwood, *Modern Caricaturists*, London, Lovat Dickson, 1932.

41. *Evening Standard*, 23 December 1929; *The Millgate*, April 1933.

42. *Nation and Athenaeum*, 28 July 1928.

43. *Listener*, 2 December 1943; unpublished notes on the history of caricature.

44. Beerbohm to Low, 18 February 1931.

45. Notes for speech at opening of exhibition by New Zealand artists at New Zealand House, London, no date (1930s?).

46. *The Home* (Australia), 2 March 1931.

47. Quoted in *John Bull*, 18 February 1950.

48. *LA*, p. 143.

49. *Ye Madde Designer*, p. 12.

50. *Spectator*, 14 May 1937.

51. *Observer*, 18 September 1927; letter to *Review of Reviews*, 8 July 1928.

CHAPTER III

1. See e.g., *John Bull*, 18 February 1950; *Illustrated*, 4 February 1950.

2. Lord Kinross (Patrick Balfour) in *Illustrated*, 4 February 1950.

3. Notes for *Sermons by Artists*; *New York Times Magazine*, 1956 (undated).

4. *LA*, pp. 39–40.

5. *Ibid.*, pp. 351–2.

6. *Ibid.*, pp. 20, 43–4.

7. *Bulletin*, 23 October 1919.

8. *Daily Herald*, 25 April 1950.

9. *New York Times Magazine*, 2 April 1961.

10. *Observer*, 18 September 1927.

11. *Listener*, 2 December 1943.

12. *LA*, p. 250; *London Calling* (BBC), No. 244, 1944.

13. Low to Herbert Morrison, 2 February 1937.

14. *Listener*, 13 February 1941; *Illustrated*, 4 February 1950.

15. *New York Times Magazine*, 1956 (undated), 2 April 1961.

16. *LA*, pp. 171–2; 'As Others See Us', manuscript dated 8 May 1952; Low to Laski, 16 November 1948.

17. Notes on democracy, Low Papers; *New York Times Magazine*, 30 October 1949.

18. *New York Times Magazine*, 18 October 1953; *Bulletin*, 23 October 1919.

19. *LA*, p. 324.

20. Unpublished manuscript, 1943, Low Papers.

21. *Economist*, 9 July 1949.

22. *LA*, pp. 201ff; *New Yorker*, 13 July 1957.

23. *LA*, p. 202.

24. Lecture notes dated 24 June 1935, Low Papers; *LA*, p. 283.

25. *Bulletin*, 23 October 1919; *Listener*, 13 February 1941.

26. *Listener*, (?) June 1941.

27. *LA*, p. 234.

28. *New Statesman*, 8 December 1956.

29. *LA*, p. 306.

CHAPTER IV

1. Jones to Low, 15 June 1949.

2. Pares to Low, 24 August 1941; Laski to Low; 11 March 1945.

Bibliography

Books and Articles by David Low

I. BOOKS

This list includes all the books authored or co-authored by David Low and the principal books to which he contributed. It excludes foreign editions, except where there was no English edition, and books using an occasional Low drawing as an illustration.

Low's Annual, 1908.

Caricatures (Sydney, Tyrrell, 1915).

With Scott – The Silver Lining (London, Smith Elder, 1916). By Griffith Taylor, with 5 illustrations by Low.

The Billy Book (Sydney, Bookstall, 1918).

Old Seed on New Ground (London, Putnam, 1920). By James Adderley, with 12 illustrations by Low.

Lloyd George & Co. (London, Allen & Unwin, 1921). Cartoons from the *Star*, with a preface by Arnold Bennett.

Man, the Lord of Creation (London, Putnam, 1920).

Low and I (London, Methuen, 1923). By F. W. Thomas, illustrated by Low.

The Low and I Holiday Book (London, Daily News, 1925). By F. W. Thomas, illustrated by Low.

Sketches by Low (London, New Statesman, 1926). Folio of 20 portraits.

Lions and Lambs (London, Jonathan Cape, 1928). 36 portraits, with interpretations by 'Lynx' (Rebecca West).

(*New Statesman* portraits of 1926 with 16 new ones.)

Hop of the Bulletin (Sydney, Angus & Robertson, 1929). By D. J. Hopkins, with 9 illustrations by Low.

The Autocracy of Mr Parham (London, Heinemann, 1930). By H. G. Wells, with 10 illustrations by Low.

The Best of Low (London, Jonathan Cape, 1930). Text and cartoons by Low.

Low's Russian Sketchbook (London, Gollancz, 1932). Text by Kingsley Martin, with 56 drawings by Low.

Modern Caricaturists (London, Lovat Dickson, 1932). By H. R. Westwood, with foreword by Low.

Caricatures by Low (London, New Statesman & Nation, 1933). Folio of 12 portraits, with biographies.

Sermons by Artists (London, Golden Cockerel Press, 1934). Includes a chapter by Low.

Low and Terry (London, Hutchinson, 1934). By Horace Thorogood and Low, with an introduction by W. W. Jacobs.

The Modern Rake's Progress

(London, Hutchinson, 1934). Text by Rebecca West, with 12 coloured illustrations by Low.

Ye Madde Designer (London, Studio, 1935). Text and illustrations by Low.

Low's Political Parade (London, Cresset Press, 1936). Text and cartoons by Low.

This England (London, New Statesman, 1937). Illustrated by Low.

Low Again (London, Cresset Press, 1938). Text and cartoons by Low.

A Cartoon History of Our Times (New York, Simon & Schuster, 1939). Text by Quincy Howe, with cartoons by Low.

This England (London, New Statesman, 1940). Illustrated by Low.

Europe since Versailles (London, Penguin Books, 1940). Text and cartoons by Low.

The Flying Visit (London, Jonathan Cape, 1940). By Peter Fleming, with illustrations by Low.

Europe at War (London, Penguin Books, 1941). Text and cartoons by Low.

Low on the War: A Cartoon Commentary of the Years 1939–41 (New York, Simon & Schuster, 1941). Text and cartoons by Low.

Low's War Cartoons (London, Cresset Press, 1941). Text and cartoons by Low.

The World at War (London, Penguin Books, 1941). Text and cartoons by Low.

British Cartoonists, Caricaturists and Comic Artists (London, Collins, 1942). Text by Low.

Jesters in Earnest (London, John Murray, 1944). Cartoons by five Czechoslovak artists ('Z.K.', A. Hoffmeister, A. Pelc, 'Stephen', W. Trier), with a preface by Low.

C'est la Guerre (London, New Europe Publishing Co., 1945). Cartoons by Low.

Valka Zacalka Mnichovem (London, New Europe Publishing Co., 1945). Cartoons by Low.

The Saturday Book, 5th year (London, Hutchinson, 1945). Contains 12 portraits by Low, with a 'Letter to Low' by Dilys Powell.

13 Jahre Weltgeschehen (Zürich, Atlantis, 1946). Cartoons by Low.

Years of Wrath: A Cartoon History 1931–45 (New York, Simon & Schuster, 1946). Text by Quincy Howe, with cartoons by Low.

Low (Copenhagen, Thaning and Appels, 1947).

Lows Kleine Weltgeschichte (Germany, Rowohlt, 1949). Cartoons by Low.

Years of Wrath: A Cartoon History 1932–45 (London, Gollancz, 1949). Text and cartoons by Low.

Low's Company (London, Methuen, 1952). 50 portraits (8 of them from *The Saturday Book* of 1945) with verses by Helen Spalding and L. A. G. Strong.

Low's Cartoon History 1945–53 (New York, Simon & Schuster, 1953). Text and cartoons by Low.

Low Visibility: A Cartoon History 1945–53 (London, Collins, 1953). Text and cartoons by Low.

Low's Autobiography (London, Michael Joseph, 1956).

The Fearful Fifties: A History of the Decade (London, Bodley Head, 1960). Text and cartoons by Low.

2. ARTICLES

This list includes articles substantially concerned with cartoon and caricature. Most of Low's articles in the *New York Times Magazine* and his wartime broadcasts published in the *Listener* were on other subjects.

'Adventures with my Pencil', *Strand Magazine*, September 1926.

'The Caricaturist's Corner', *Nation & Athenaeum*, 28 July 1928.

'The Art of Max Beerbohm', *Spectator*, 14 February 1931.

'To One of my so-called Victims', *Listener*, 21 December 1932.

'Bereavement of Colonel Blimp', *Listener*, 26 August 1936.

'The Changing Face of Humour', *Listener*, 8 December 1938.

'The Cartoonist's Job in War', *Listener*, 2 November 1939.

'Art & Propaganda', with Eric Newton and J. L. Beddington, *Listener*, 15 February 1940.

'Leonardo da Disney', *New Republic*, 5 January 1942.

'Was Colonel Blimp Right?', *Evening Standard*, 14 October 1942.

'As One Caricaturist to Another: An Imaginary Interview Between David Low & James Gillray', *Listener*, 2 December 1943.

'"Krokodil", & Russian Comic Art', *Listener*, 1 March 1951.

'Years on my Drawing Board', *New York Times*, 2 April 1961.

Other Authors

A bibliography of works mentioning David Low would include virtually every general discussion of British cartoon and caricature since about 1920. Below are listed a few noteworthy but generally ephemeral items, not all of which have been cited in the text.

Blunt, Anthony. 'Imaginative Humour', *Spectator*, 14 May 1937.

Lawlor, Pat. 'The Early Drawings of David Low', *The Turnbull Library Record*, Vol. 4, July–December 1941.

Mellini, Peter. 'Colonel Blimp's England', *History Today*, Vol. 34, October 1984.

Nash, Paul. 'British Humorous

Draughtsmen', *Week-End Review*, 18 July 1931.

Picture Post. 'David Low', 22 October 1938.

Pritchett, V. S. 'The Manhandling Democratic Touch', *New Yorker*, 13 April 1957.

Searle, Ronald. 'Master of English Caricature', *Guardian*, 21 September 1963.

Streicher, L. H. 'David Low & the Sociology of Caricature', *Comparative Studies in Society and History*, Vol. 8, 1965–66.

Westwood, H. R. *Modern Caricaturists*, (London, Lovat Dickson, 1932).

Picture Sources and Acknowledgements

Low's method and technique varied little after he had achieved his mature style. Nearly all his cartoons for the *Evening Standard*, *Daily Herald* and *Guardian* are brushed in black ink on sheets of high-quality rag paper 18 × 24 in (46 × 60 cm). Drawings for the *Star* (1919–27) have largely disappeared, perhaps as the result of fire at a storage warehouse. The few that remain tend to be smaller, averaging 12 × 10 in (31 × 26 cm). Low's Australian work for the *Bulletin* was drawn on card, usually about 24 × 18 in (60 × 48 cm), though the column-filler caricatures averaged 12 × 10 in (31 × 26 cm). The change from pen work to brush (probably sable size 3, 4 or 5, in the main) occurred over a period of a couple of years around 1915–16. The famous 'Imperial Conference' cartoon ('Talk to him in Welsh, David . . .', 1916) is one of Low's last works drawn completely with a pen. Thereafter, Low worked only with pencil and brush. His *New Statesman* caricatures were carefully modelled with a soft pencil to imitate a lithographic crayon finish. For cartooning, however, he always covered the softer, naturalistic pencil sketch with his sharp, definitive inked brush.

The main publicly accessible collections of Low's drawings are:

Alexander Turnbull Library, Wellington, New Zealand: 85 original drawings, including New Zealand politicians.
Australian National Library, Canberra: 54 original drawings donated by Low.
Centre for the Study of Cartoons and Caricature, University of Kent at Canterbury: 3,145 original drawings for the *Evening Standard* 1927–50.
National Portrait Gallery, London: 18 original drawings, including a self-portrait in oils. There are also over 100 sketchbook pages.
New Zealand High Commission, London: 50 original drawings, a sketchbook and a complete selection of Low's published books.
State Library of New South Wales, Mitchell Library, Sydney: 283 original drawings mainly for the *Bulletin* 1911–19.

For assistance in supplying cartoons and/or for permission to reproduce them, the authors wish to thank the following:

The Low family: nos. 1, 2, 3, 4, 5, 13, 18, 19, 20, 21, 25, 27, 29, 31, 34, 35, 39, 40, 52, 53, 57, 70, 73, 74, 76, 80, 81, 87, 88, 111, 114, 115, 118, 119, 120, 121, 122, 123, 124, 129, 130, 131, 143, 147, 152, 154, 158; Express News and Features Service, London and the Low family: nos. 22, 23, 28, 30, 32, 33, 36, 38, 41, 44, 45, 46, 47, 48, 50, 51, 54, 55, 56, 58, 59, 61, 62, 65, 66, 67, 71, 72, 75, 82, 83, 84, 85, 86, 89, 90, 91, 92, 93, 94, 95, 96, 97, 99, 100, 101, 102, 103, 104, 105, 106, 107, 108, 110, 116, 117, 125, 126, 127, 128, 132, 133, 134, 135, 136, 137, 139, 140, 142, 145, 146, 150, 151, 153, 155, 156, 157; Centre for the Study of Cartoons and Caricature, University of Kent at Canterbury: nos. 44, 45, 47, 49, 50, 51, 54, 55, 56, 59, 61, 62, 65, 66, 67, 75, 82, 83, 84, 85, 89, 90, 91, 92, 97, 99, 102, 105, 106, 107, 108, 110, 127, 128, 132, 135, 136, 137, 140, 145, 146, 150, 151, 155, 156, 157; London School of Economics and Political Science: nos. 24, 42, 63, 98, 109, 113, 138, 148, 149; State Library of New South Wales, Mitchell Library, Sydney: nos. 7, 8, 9a, 9b, 12, 60; Australian National Library, Canberra: nos. 14, 15, 16, 26, 64, 112; Australian Consolidated Press (the *Bulletin*): nos. 6, 10; British Museum: nos. 37, 68; British Library, Newspaper Section: no. 17; Art Gallery of South Australia, Adelaide: no. 11; National Portrait Gallery, London: no. 141; Paul Duffell & Terence Fisher Collection: no. 142; Mr and Mrs George G. Walker: no. 43; private collection: nos. 69, 77, 78, 79; John C. Wallace: no. 144; *New Statesman and Nation*: title page

The Authors have attempted to trace all copyright holders. Advice of omissions would be appreciated and they will be corrected in future editions.

Index

All numbers refer to pages. Roman numbers refer to text; italic numbers to illustrations.